Complete
ScienceSmart®

Grade **5**

Andrea Berlin Philp

Credits

Photos (Front Cover "satellite dish" David Hughes/123RF.com, "gears" alex_star/123RF.com, "jet plane" Lars Christenen/123RF.com.
Back Cover "girl on left"/123RF.com, "boy" Jose Manuel Gelpi Diaz/123RF.com, "girl in middle"/123RF.com,
"girl on right" Paul Hakimata/123RF.com, "memo board" Sandra Van Der Steen/123RF.com, "children"/123RF.com.)

ISBN: 978-1-897457-77-1

Table of Contents

Section 1 — Understanding Life Systems

Students will understand that the human body is made up of a number of organs that work together in different systems. They will learn about the structures and functions of the digestive, skeletal, respiratory, circulatory, and nervous systems. They will be able to identify the major organs and parts of these systems, and examine how they work. In addition, students will investigate the effects of some social and environmental factors on their health. They will also learn to make healthy choices in their daily lives.

ISBN 978-1-897457-77-1

Understanding Structures and Mechanisms

Students will examine the impacts of external forces, caused by natural occurrences and human activities, on structures, and investigate how structures can be strengthened. They will also explore how different types of internal and external forces act on structures, like different types of bridges in particular. In addition, students will discover how simple machines work together to make mechanical systems and how these systems provide mechanical advantages. They will also understand how protective equipment protects people during certain activities.

ISBN: 978-1-897457-77-1

Table of Contents

Section 3

Understanding Matter and Energy

Students will explore the properties of matter and the characteristics of the three states of matter, as well as the different ways of measuring and describing matter. They will examine how heat changes the states of matter, which are either physical or chemical changes, and learn that these changes can be reversible or irreversible. Moreover, students will investigate the environmental impacts of the production, use, and disposal of different materials.

ISBN: 978-1-897457-77-1

Understanding Earth and Space Systems

Students will learn about the different forms of energy and how they are used in their everyday lives. They will investigate the various energy sources and understand that these sources are either renewable or non-renewable. Moreover, they will explore the transformation of energy from one form to another. The impacts of energy use on the environment will also be studied. In addition, students will understand the importance of conserving energy and learn ways to reduce energy consumption.

ISBN: 978-1-897457-77-1

ISBN: 978-1-897457-77-1

Understanding
Life Systems

ISBN: 978-1-897457-77-1

1 Digestive System

Your digestive system breaks down the food you eat. It also gets rid of things that your body does not need as waste. In this unit, you will explore the journey your food takes in the digestive system.

After completing this unit, you will

- know the functions of the digestive system.
- know the parts of the digestive system.
- understand how the digestive system works.

Mom, I know that I should chew more. It can help lighten the load of my digestive system.

nutrient-rich foods

Vocabulary

nutrient: something that the body needs to live, grow, and stay healthy

enzyme: a chemical that helps break down food

Chewing is the first step in digesting food. Each part of your mouth – the tongue, salivary glands, and teeth – plays an important role in the process of chewing. Your tongue not only moves the food around the mouth to help your teeth do their job, but it also enables you to taste food. Taste buds on the tip of the tongue, for example, help detect sweetness in food. Put a candy on either side of your tongue to see whether you can taste the sweetness.

A. Fill in the blanks and boxes with the given words.

Digestive System

function	nutrients	food
waste	breaks	organs

The digestive system is a system of 1. _organs_ that processes the food you eat and 2. _breaks_ it down into the nutrients that your body needs to 3. _waste_ and grow. After digestion, waste materials are removed from your body.

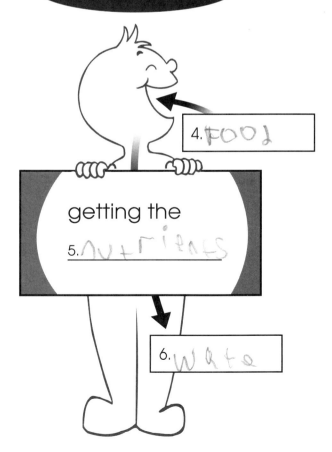

4. _FOOd_

getting the
5. _Nutrients_

6. _Wate_

B. Label the parts of the digestive system. Then fill in the blanks to show the journey of an apple as it is eaten and digested.

Parts of the Digestive System

swallow   stomach   mouth   large

waste   water   nutrients   saliva

esophagus   rectum

rectum   small intestine   mouth

colon   stomach   esophagus

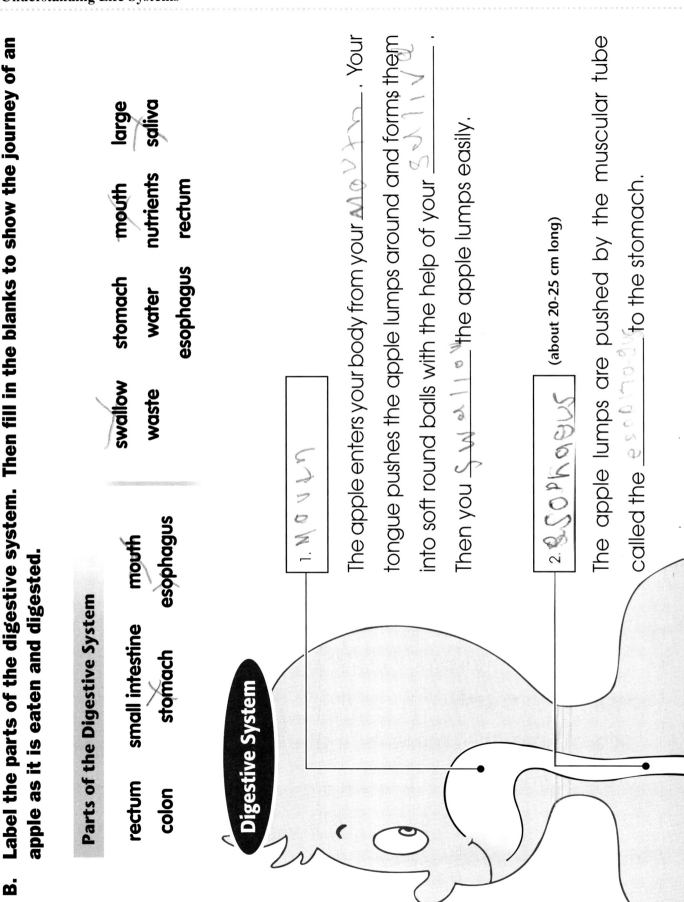

Digestive System

1. Mouth

The apple enters your body from your ~~Mouth~~. Your tongue pushes the apple lumps around and forms them into soft round balls with the help of your ~~saliva~~.

Then you ~~swallow~~ the apple lumps easily.

2. Esophagus (about 20-25 cm long)

The apple lumps are pushed by the muscular tube called the ~~esophagus~~ to the stomach.

ISBN: 978-1-897457-77-1

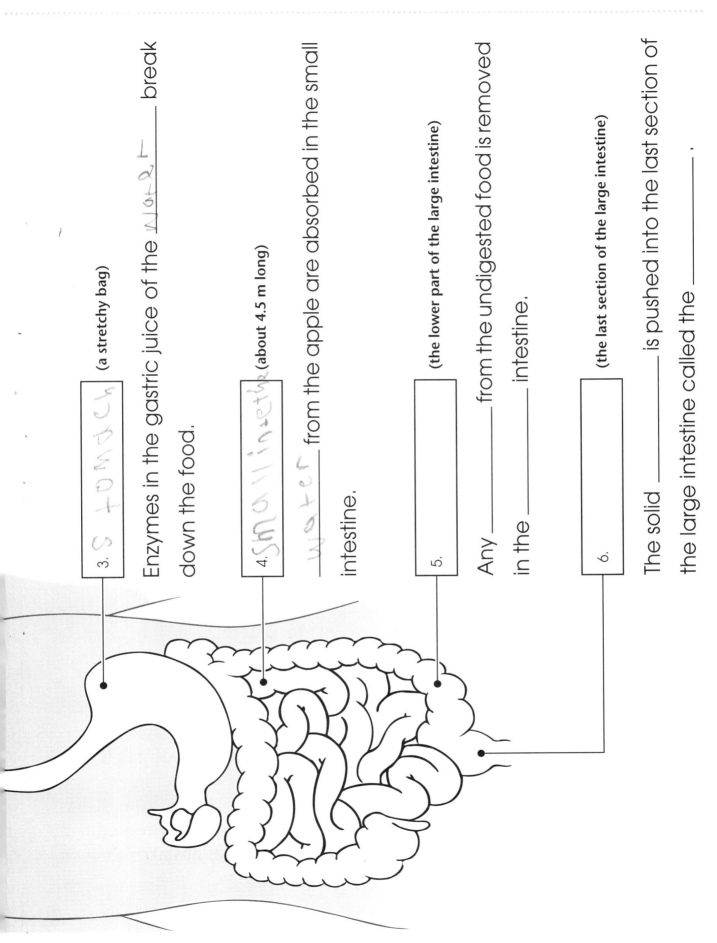

3. S tomach (a stretchy bag)

Enzymes in the gastric juice of the _Water_ break down the food.

4. Small insetih (about 4.5 m long)

Water from the apple are absorbed in the small intestine.

5. _____ (the lower part of the large intestine)

Any _____ from the undigested food is removed in the _____ intestine.

6. _____ (the last section of the large intestine)

The solid _____ is pushed into the last section of the large intestine called the _____.

ISBN: 978-1-897457-77-1

C. Read the passage. Then answer the questions.

Do Cows Have Four Stomachs?

Cows have one stomach, but it is made up of four compartments. It is this complex stomach, combined with a cow's method of chewing, that allows a cow to get the nutrients it needs from grass.

Cows are ruminants: they can digest indigestible food because they regurgitate and chew their food over and over. They chew grass, swallow it, and send it on its long journey. The journey begins in the **rumen**, where grass is partially digested by helpful bacteria. It moves on to the **reticulum**, the chamber that separates the chunks of partially digested food, "cud", into pieces small enough to move to the next chamber and pieces that need to go back to the mouth for further chewing. If the cud is small enough, it heads to the **omasum**, where water and minerals are absorbed from the cud. Finally, it goes to the **abomasum**, which is like the human stomach; it has stomach juices and is attached to the intestines. By the time the cud reaches the intestines, the cow's body has absorbed enough nutrients to stay healthy and strong.

ISBN: 978-1-897457-77-1

1. How many stomachs does a cow have? Explain.

   _____

   _____

2. Cows are ruminants. What are ruminants?

   _____

   _____

3. Label the parts of a cow's stomach with the help of the words in bold in the passage. Then complete the descriptions.

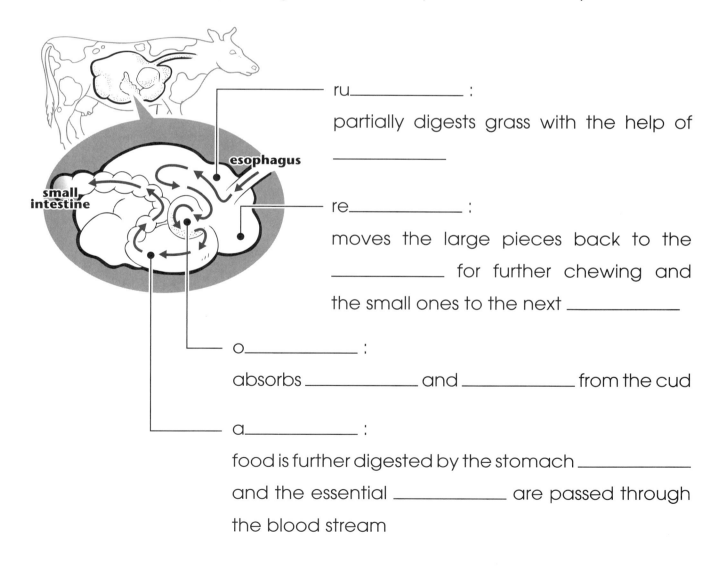

ru_____ :
partially digests grass with the help of

_____

re_____ :
moves the large pieces back to the _____ for further chewing and the small ones to the next _____

o_____ :
absorbs _____ and _____ from the cud

a_____ :
food is further digested by the stomach _____ and the essential _____ are passed through the blood stream

2 Skeletal System

Under our skin, along with organs and muscles, we have bones. These bones form the skeletal system. In this unit, you will look at what a bone is made up of. You will also learn about the role of the skeletal system and identify the parts.

break

EYE ANATOMY

HUMA

Like your skin, your bone will heal itself. Meanwhile, wear this cast for extra protection.

After completing this unit, you will

- know the functions of the skeletal system.
- know the structure of bones.
- be able to identify some bones in the skeletal system.

Vocabulary

cartilage: a flexible tissue that can be found in joints

joint: the place where two bones meet

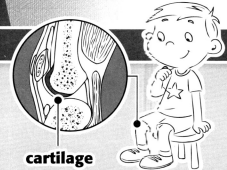

cartilage

You know that your ears are soft and flexible. However, have you ever wondered what your ears have that gives them their shape and structure? Cartilage is what you have in your ears. It is a flexible tissue which is lighter than bone but can still provide structure. This is why your ears can hold their shape and stay flexible at the same time. After all, you had more cartilage than bones when you were in your mother's womb. By the time you are about 25, most of this cartilage will become bone.

Can you name another body part that also has cartilage?

A. Check the correct circles to show the functions of bones.

Functions of Our Skeletal System

You have 4 functions.

- (A) provides body structure
- (B) adds weight to your body
- (C) protects organs
- (D) protects skin
- (E) creates nutrients
- (F) makes new blood cells
- (G) allows for body movement along with muscles

ISBN: 978-1-897457-77-1

B. **Label the diagram to show the inside of a bone and our skeletal system. Then fill in the blanks.**

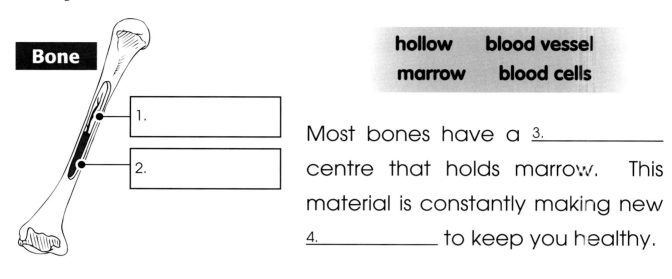

hollow	blood vessel
marrow	blood cells

Most bones have a 3._____ centre that holds marrow. This material is constantly making new 4._____ to keep you healthy.

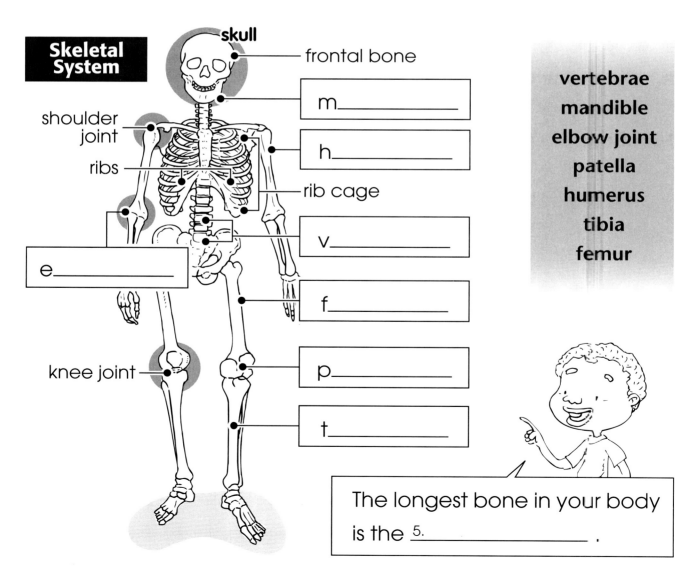

vertebrae
mandible
elbow joint
patella
humerus
tibia
femur

The longest bone in your body is the 5._____ .

C.   Look at the diagrams on the previous page. Answer the questions.

1.   What protects your brain and gives your face its shape?

_____

2.   What protects your heart and lungs?

_____

3.   Name two joints in your body.

_____

D.   Complete the diagram with the words in bold. Then answer the questions.

1.

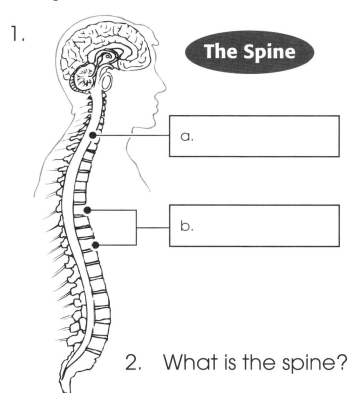

The Spine

a. _____

b. _____

The spine is a column of bones that runs down your back. The bones in the spine are called **vertebrae**. Your spine helps hold up your body and protects a bundle of nerves called the **spinal cord**.

2.   What is the spine?

_____

3.   What are the functions of the spine?

_____

_____

E. Read the passage. Then answer the questions.

How do bones grow? Special bone cells do most of the work. Osteoblasts make new bone tissue so that bones can grow and repair themselves. Osteoclasts break down old bone tissue. When you are young, osteoblasts out-work osteoclasts, but as you age, it is the other way around. Your bones get weaker and smaller as you get older.

How does a broken bone heal? When a bone breaks, blood vessels inside the bone break, too. Blood rushing out of the vessels clots, which means the blood sticks together and hardens, making the area swell; this clotted blood acts as glue while the bone repairs itself. Within a week, new bone starts to grow. Within a few weeks, the broken ends have grown together. For a while, the repaired bone is extra-thick because it is made of both old and new bone. However, after several months, repaired bone is back to its original thickness. All of this happens naturally; you only wear a cast to protect new bone, which is weak during this process.

BONES:
Growing, Breaking, and Repairing

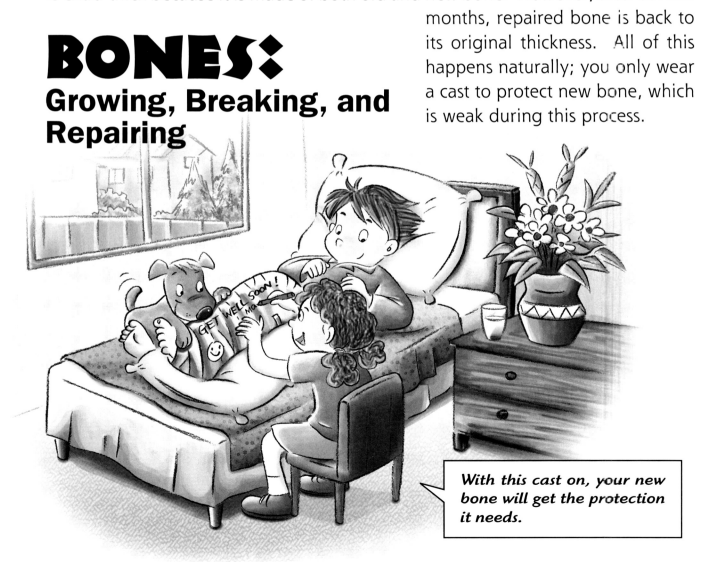

With this cast on, your new bone will get the protection it needs.

ISBN: 978-1-897457-77-1

1. Write the function of each type of bone cell. Then write "osteoblasts" or "osteoclasts" in the boxes.

a. Osteoblasts: _____

b. Osteoclasts: _____

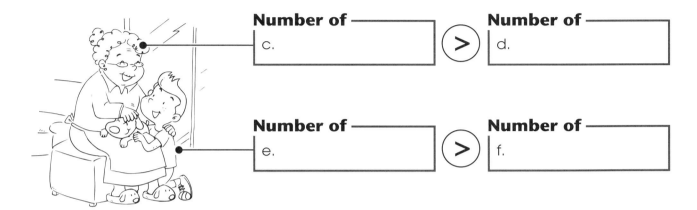

Number of ——————
c.

>

Number of ——————
d.

Number of ——————
e.

>

Number of ——————
f.

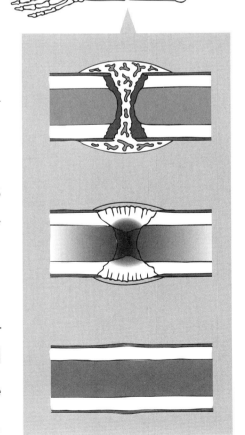

Bone Repair

2. Complete the descriptions.

a. Swelling occurs because _____ sticks and hardens around the break.

b. Within a week, new _____ starts to grow. The broken ends will grow together after several weeks.

c. The repaired bone is _____ because it is made of both old and new bone. After several months, the bone returns to its original _____ .

ISBN: 978-1-897457-77-1

3 Respiratory System

We can live without food and water for a few days. However, without air, we only last a very short time. In this unit, you will identify the respiratory organs and look at the cycle of the respiratory system.

> *Teddy, we need air. Don't you think that it is nice to breathe in fresh air?*

> *It smells good...*

After completing this unit, you will

- know the structure of the lungs and their functions.
- be able to identify the parts of the respiratory system.
- understand how the respiratory system works.

inhale: breathe in

exhale: breathe out

oxygen: a gas that our bodies need

carbon dioxide: a gas that our bodies produce and expel

oxygen

carbon dioxide

ISBN: 978-1-897457-77-1

So you know what boogers are – the little blobs that are inside your nose. However, before these blobs became what they are, they were a sticky and slimy substance, which we call mucus. The air that you breathe in contains lots of dust and dirt which your lungs do not want. Mucus helps you get rid of them. It traps the tiny things in the air by getting them to stick to it. Then, the filtered air enters your body. When dirty mucus dries, it becomes the boogers in your nose.

You should never pick your nose. Blow it with a tissue instead.

A. Look at the lungs, the major organ in your respiratory system. Then fill in the blanks.

bigger	two	three
lobes	rib cage	left

right   left

The Lungs

We have 1._____ lungs. They are protected by the 2._____ . Each lung is made up of different sections called 3._____ . The right lung has 4._____ lobes and the 5._____ lung has two lobes. The right lung is a little 6._____ than the left lung.

B. Label the respiratory organs. Then fill in the blanks to complete the descriptions.

respiratory organs

| diaphragm | trachea | bronchiole | larynx | nasal cavity |

| bronchial tubes | cleaned | lungs | muscle | tube |

Respiratory System

bronchial tubes

alveoli: air sacs at the end of a bronchiole

1. _____ :

a place where air is warmed and
2._____ before entering the body

3. _____ :

a short 4._____ that is located in
the throat and helps us make sounds

5. _____ :

known as the windpipe; air flows
through it to the 6._____

7. _____ :

the minor air passages at the ends of
the 8._____ which lead oxygen
into the lungs

9. _____ :

the strong 10._____ at the
bottom of the lungs

ISBN 978-1-897457-77-1

C. **Write the respiratory organs in the boxes and colour the arrows to complete the cycle of the respiratory system. Then answer the question.**

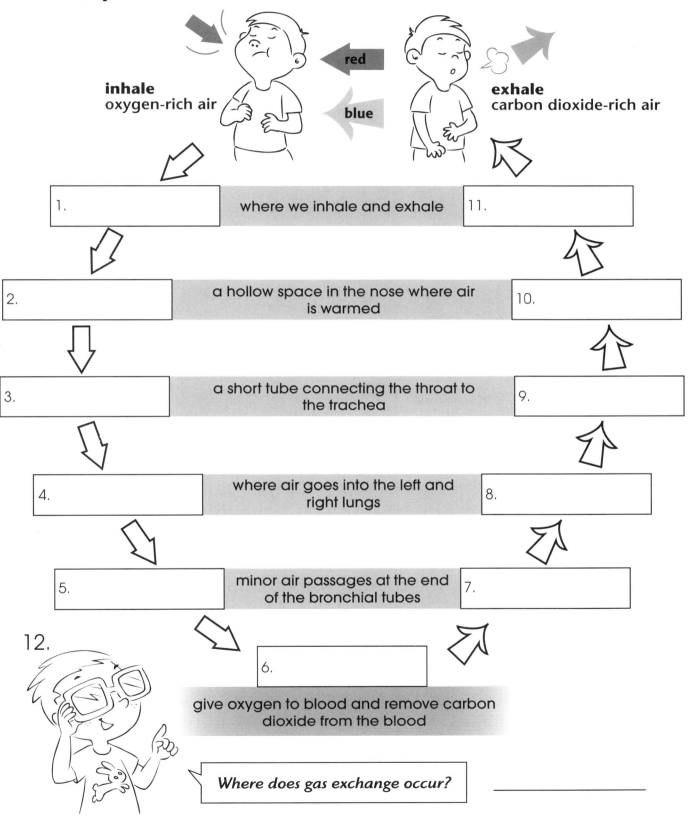

inhale
oxygen-rich air

red

blue

exhale
carbon dioxide-rich air

| 1. | where we inhale and exhale | 11. |

| 2. | a hollow space in the nose where air is warmed | 10. |

| 3. | a short tube connecting the throat to the trachea | 9. |

| 4. | where air goes into the left and right lungs | 8. |

| 5. | minor air passages at the end of the bronchial tubes | 7. |

12.

| 6. |

give oxygen to blood and remove carbon dioxide from the blood

Where does gas exchange occur? _____

D. Read the passage. Label the parts of each animal. Then complete the descriptions and colour the arrows.

Respiration:
Not Just a Job for the Lungs

Dad, do you think we could live in the water one day?

Gills, not lungs, are the site of gas exchange for many aquatic animals, such as fish. Fish get oxygen to their gills by drinking water, which contains dissolved oxygen. The water flows across their fleshy, sheet-like gills. This allows the oxygen in the water to diffuse into the blood circulating through the gills' blood vessels. As the oxygen moves into the blood, carbon dioxide from the blood moves into the water. Then, water with dissolved carbon dioxide leaves the body via flaps, called opercula (singular: operculum), at the side of the fish's head.

Not all animals that breathe underwater use gills. Frogs have lungs much like humans, which they use when they are on land, but when they are underwater, they breathe through their skin. Like fish, they extract dissolved oxygen from water and expel carbon dioxide into the water, but they do this directly through their skin, which is full of tiny blood vessels where gas exchange occurs.

ISBN 978-1-897457-77-1

red ➤ : oxygen-rich air   blue ➤ : oxygen-poor air

1.

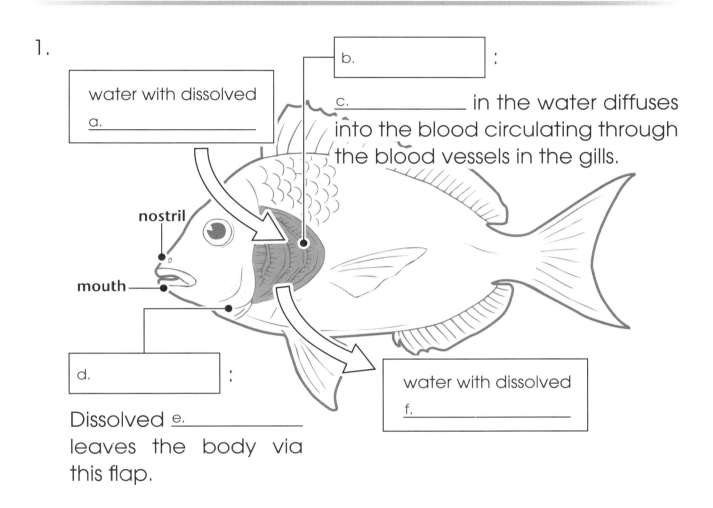

b. _____ :

c. _____ in the water diffuses into the blood circulating through the blood vessels in the gills.

water with dissolved
a. _____

nostril

mouth

d. _____ :

Dissolved e. _____ leaves the body via this flap.

water with dissolved
f. _____

2.

nostril

mouth

lungs

Frogs use their a. _____ to breathe when they are on land, and they can breathe in water through their b. _____ .

ISBN: 978-1-897457-77-1

Experiment

Introduction

Lung capacity is the maximum amount of air a person's lungs can hold. This amount increases as we become more physically active. In this experiment, you will investigate how much air you can hold.

Hypothesis

My lungs can hold _____ mL of air.

Steps

1. Fill the bottle with water and close the cap.

2. Fill the sink with water.

3. Turn the bottle upside down and lower it into the sink. Then remove the cap carefully and make sure no air can go into the bottle.

Materials

- *an empty 2-L bottle*
- *a measuring cup*
- *a clean plastic tube*
- *a marker*

ISBN 978-1-897457-77-1

4. Insert the end of the tube into the bottle while keeping the bottle under water.

Ask an adult to hold the bottle for you.

5. Take a deep breath and blow into the tube.

6. Mark the water level on the bottle after you breathe out.

Empty the bottle and fill it with water up to the mark.

7. Then pour the water out from the bottle to a measuring cup. This represents the volume of air that you can hold.

Result

My Lung Capacity: _____ mL

Conclusion

The hypothesis was: _____

_____

My experiment _____ the hypothesis.
supported/did not support

4 Circulatory System

The circulatory system is like your body's highway. Along this highway, the heart, the blood, and the blood vessels work together to move many substances through your body. In this unit, you will examine how the circulatory system works.

After completing this unit, you will

- be able to identify the parts of the heart.
- understand how the circulatory system works.

Doctor, is it true that you can tell how healthy my brother's heart is by listening to his heartbeat with your stethoscope?

Vocabulary

heart: an organ that pumps blood

arteries: the blood vessels that carry blood from the heart to the body

veins: the blood vessels that carry blood back to the heart

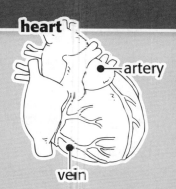

ISBN 978-1-897457-77-1

You can feel my pulse easily on the wrist where there is a big blood vessel.

Your heart is a strong muscle that works like a pump. As the muscle contracts, it squeezes blood out and around your body. Each contraction is called a heartbeat. Try to find a pulse point and feel your heartbeat. You will realize that your heart beats at a steady rate. When you exercise, you may feel that your heart beats faster than usual.

A. Name the parts of the circulatory system and complete their descriptions.

The Circulatory System

blood	arteries	heart	back
away	nutrients	fist	veins

- h_____ : size of a _____ ; pumps blood

- a_____ : tubes that carry blood _____ from the heart

- v_____ : tubes that carry blood _____ to the heart

- b_____ : delivers essential _____ and oxygen

B. Fill in the blanks to complete the paragraph about the heart.

There are ___1._____ chambers in the heart. The right side of the heart has a right ___2._____ and a right ___3._____ . The left atrium and left ventricle are on the ___4._____ side of the heart. ___5._____ open to let blood flow between the chambers in the correct directions.

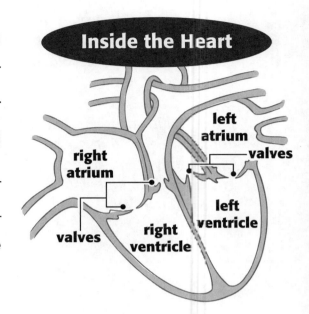

C. Fill in the blanks to complete the diagram. Then fill in the correct words to show how the circulatory system works.

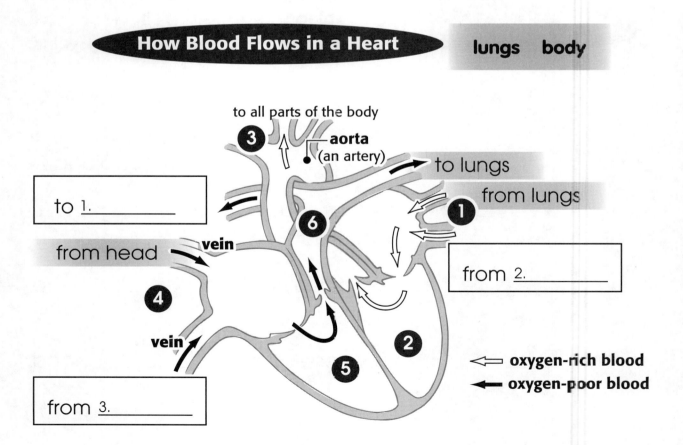

Circulatory System

Oxygen-rich blood

① The oxygen-4._____ blood from the lungs enters the left 5._____ and goes to the left ventricle through a 6._____ .

② The left ventricle pumps blood out through another 7._____ .

③ The 8._____ , which is the main artery, branches into smaller arteries that carry blood to all parts of the body.

Oxygen-poor blood

④ 9._____ carry the oxygen-poor blood from the head and body back to the heart. The blood flows into the right 10._____ .

⑤ The blood goes to the 11._____ ventricle.

⑥ The right ventricle pumps the blood to the 12._____ .

The blood leaves 13._____ in the lungs and picks up oxygen. Veins from the lungs bring blood carrying 14._____ back to the heart.

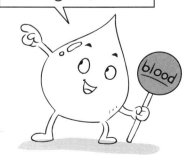

The cycle starts all over again!

ISBN: 978-1-897457-77-1

Complete ScienceSmart • **Grade 5**   **31**

To Replace a Broken Heart

D. Read the passage. Then answer the questions.

Transplant surgery is an amazing feat. First, a team of surgeons removes a patient's sick heart, and the patient is put on a cardiopulmonary bypass machine – or heart-lung machine – which acts as the patient's heart and lungs during surgery. Then, a new, healthy heart, donated by an organ donor (someone who has agreed to donate his or her organs after death), is placed inside the patient. Finally, the surgeons start the new heart and take the patient off the heart-lung machine.

The first successful heart transplant was performed in South Africa in December 1967; the first in the United States was performed in January 1968; and the first in Canada was performed in May 1968. All of the patients died soon after their surgeries, as early transplant surgery had one big problem: people's bodies rejected their new hearts. It was not until the 1980s that patients could expect to live for years after their heart transplants. In fact, the first successful heart transplant on a child was performed in the United States in 1984 and the patient is still alive today!

ISBN: 978-1-897457-77-1

A Cardiopulmonary Bypass Machine for Transplant Surgeries

1. Common name: _____ machine

2. Function: It pumps the blood throughout the rest of the body, removing **carbon dioxide / oxygen** and replacing it with **oxygen / carbon dioxide** needed by body tissues.

3. When to use: Once the **sick / healthy** heart is removed, the patient is put on this machine. When a new, healthy heart donated by an organ **donor / maker** is placed inside the patient, the patient is taken off the machine.

Timeline of Heart Transplant
The first successful heart transplant...

1968

Nov
Dec — performed in 4. _____

Jan — performed in 5. _____

Feb

Mar — performed in 6. _____

April

May

Jun

:(All of the patients 7. _____ soon after the surgeries due to rejection.

1984 — performed in 8. _____ on a 9. _____

:) The patient is still 10. _____ !

5 Nervous System

Your brain, along with your nerves and spinal cord, make up your nervous system. In this unit, you will learn the parts of the nervous system and their functions.

After completing this unit, you will

- be able to identify the parts of the nervous system.
- know the function of each part of the nervous system.
- know the function of each part of the brain.

Mom, I'm sure Baby Sam has a well-developed brain because he learned to build a tower in seconds.

brain

Vocabulary

brain: the organ that controls the body

nerves: pathways that send messages from the brain to the body

spinal cord: a bundle of nerves that connects the brain and the nerve cells

Humans have the largest brain of all animals in proportion to their body size.

 ISBN: 978-1-897457-77-1

Extension

One of the functions of your brain is to send messages to your body so that your body reacts. A good example is the brain freeze that you get from eating ice cream. When the ice cream touches the nerves at the roof of your mouth, these nerves will send a message to your brain telling it that the area is cold. The brain gets the impression that the environment is cold, hence, it sends a message back demanding more blood flow to warm itself up. This sudden increase of blood supply causes the blood vessels to swell, which makes your head feel like it is pounding.

Eat your ice cream slowly to prevent brain freeze.

A. Label the diagram of the nervous system and circle the correct answers.

The Nervous System

nerves   brain   spinal cord

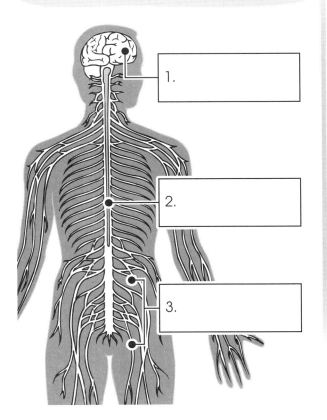

1. _____
2. _____
3. _____

The Brain

- a **soft / hard** organ

- protected by the **hair / skull**

- has a **smooth / wrinkled** surface

- weighs about **1.5 kg / 20 kg**

- our body's **control / repair** centre

B. Label the parts of the nervous system. Then fill in the blanks to complete the descriptions.

Parts of the Nervous System

cerebellum   spinal cord   coordination   biggest   memories   voluntary
cerebrum   brain stem   involuntary   spinal cord   messages   nerves

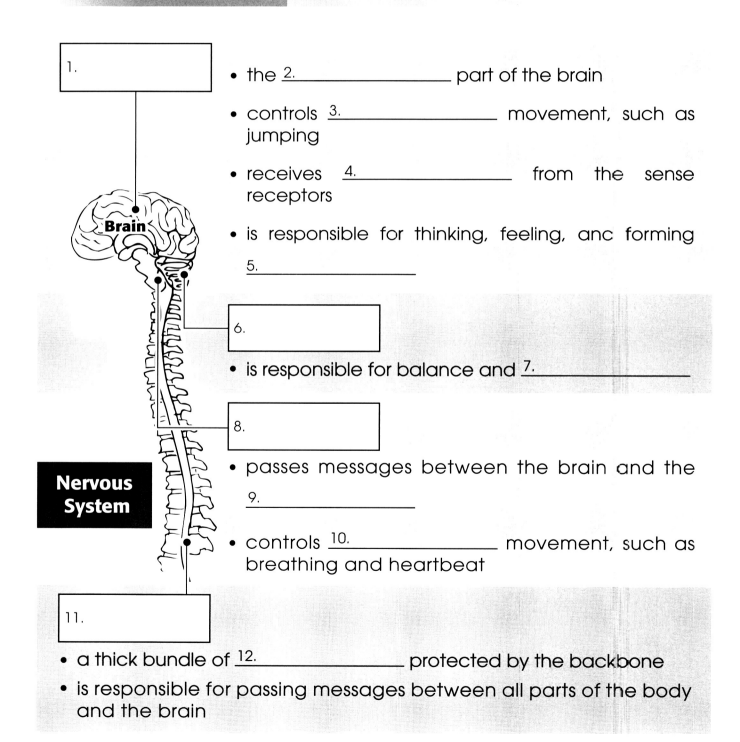

1. _____

- the 2. _____ part of the brain

- controls 3. _____ movement, such as jumping

- receives 4. _____ from the sense receptors

- is responsible for thinking, feeling, anc forming
  5. _____

Brain

6. _____

- is responsible for balance and 7. _____

8. _____

- passes messages between the brain and the
  9. _____

- controls 10. _____ movement, such as breathing and heartbeat

Nervous System

11. _____

- a thick bundle of 12. _____ protected by the backbone

- is responsible for passing messages between all parts of the body and the brain

ISBN: 378-1-897457-77-1

C. Name the three parts of a brain. Then match them with the correct functions.

Three Parts of a Brain	Functions
c_ _ _ _r_ _ •	• keeps you balanced
c_ _ _ _ _ll_ _ •	• passes messages to the spinal cord
b_ _ _ _ s_ _ _ •	• makes decisions
	• receives messages from eyes
	• controls sneezing and swallowing

D. Identify each group as "voluntary activities" or "involuntary activities". Give one more example. Then name and colour the part of the brain that is responsible for controlling the activities.

1. _____

• breathing
• vomiting
• coughing

• 2. _____

3.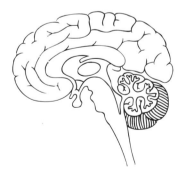

Activities are controlled by:

_____

4. _____

• working out a solution
• drawing a picture
• memorizing a formula

• 5. _____

6.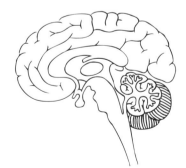

Activities are controlled by:

_____

ISBN: 978-1-397457-77-1

E. Read the passage. Trace the dotted lines to show how we react in different situations and complete the descriptions.

You probably do not like to feel pain. And that is the point. Pain is your body's way of telling you to stop doing whatever it is that is causing pain, like touching a hot stove. It is also your body's way of telling you to rest so that your body can recover from any injury you might have got. What's more, pain tells you to avoid similar painful situation in the future.

Pain is caused by stimuli like heat (a burn), external forces (banging your toe), and parts of your body (a heart attack). These stimuli activate special nerves in your skin and internal organs. In the case of touching a hot stove, the nerves in your skin send messages to your spinal cord, which almost instantaneously tells your muscles to move your hand. This quick response is called a reflex, which is something your body does without you thinking about doing it. Your brain gets the message after your body has already reacted, but it tells you to remember not to touch the hot stove again!

ISBN: 978-1-897457-77-1

Two Ways We React

1. ### The Brain Tells Muscles What to Do

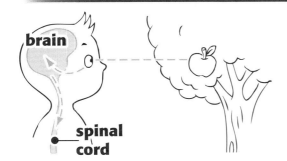
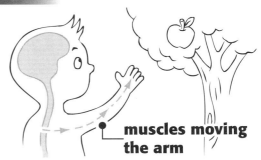

Your eyes send a message to your a. _____ . Your brain thinks and decides to get the apple. It sends a message to your b. _____ .

Your c. _____ passes the message on to your muscles. The message tells your d. _____ to move to get the apple.

2. ### A Reflex

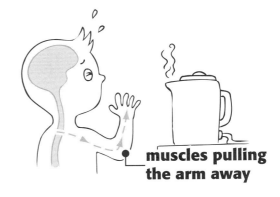

A message is sent from your fingertips to your a. _____ .

Your spinal cord sends a message back to your arm b. _____ . Your muscles pull your hand away to prevent it from being badly hurt.

c. A reflex is _____ .

6 Human Health and Diseases

Many social and environmental factors impact our health. Some factors are harmful while others are beneficial. In this unit, you will see some of these factors and learn about how they affect our health.

After completing this unit, you will

- be able to identify social factors and environmental factors.
- know the causes of some common diseases.
- know what healthy choices should be made.

The smoke from these factories has a negative impact on our health, but the trees we plant will help solve the problem.

Vocabulary

contaminate: pollute something, making it harmful if consumed

ultraviolet rays: invisible rays that come from the sun

Most contaminated food is safe to consume after it is thoroughly cooked.

ISBN: 978-1-897457-77-1

You know that trans fats are bad fats, but what makes them unhealthy? Trans fats are actually transformed from healthy fats such as vegetable oil. However, a chemical process that healthy fats go through to become solid makes them bad trans fats. Our bodies do need healthy fats, but not trans fats, to function properly. Eating trans fat can clog arteries, which can lead to strokes. It also increases the risk of heart disease by lowering "good" cholesterol and raising "bad" cholesterol. Margarines, shortenings, fried foods, and bakery products can contain these trans fats. Therefore, we should limit our intake of these foods.

Start a healthy habit – read the nutrition facts and find out how much trans fat a food product has before you eat it.

A. Label each group of factors as "social" or "environmental". Then check the activities that can have negative impacts on our health.

Negative Impacts on Our Health

1. _____ factors: caused by physical surroundings

   Ⓐ planting trees   Ⓑ factory emitting smoke

   Ⓒ spraying bug spray   Ⓓ waste gas from cars

2. _____ factors: caused by people around us

   Ⓐ people smoking in a public area

   Ⓑ waiters offering fatty food

   Ⓒ people coughing without covering their mouths

   Ⓓ posters recruiting members for a sports team

B. Fill in the blanks to learn about the common diseases. Then label the diagram with the disease names and determine the systems that they affect.

Common Diseases   hole   large   muscles   airways

epilepsy: abnormal activity in the brain causes a person to lose control of the 1._____

asthma: breathing becomes difficult as the 2._____ are swollen

appendicitis: the appendix, a small pouch connected to the 3._____ intestine, is inflamed, causing pain and cramps

atrial septal defect: a 4._____ in the heart allows oxygen-rich and oxygen-poor blood to mix

Common Diseases and Body Systems Affected

5._____ affects 6._____ system

7._____ affects 8._____ system

9._____ affects 10._____ system

11._____ affects 12._____ system

ISBN: 978-1-897457-77-1

C. Circle the correct words to show the healthy choices. Then suggest one more healthy choice.

Healthy Choices

✓ Get enough **pets / sleep** .

✓ Eat **tasty / healthy** food.

✓ Wear **protective / trendy** sports gear.

✓ Drink enough water to...

- **dehydrate / hydrate** your body.

- help your body excrete **waste / nutrients** .

✓ Apply sunscreen before sun exposure to...

- block the strong **heat / radiation** .

- avoid **skin / lung** cancer.

Be physically active to...

- strengthen your **intelligence / muscles** .

- **increase / decrease** your lung capacity.

 _____

_____

D. Read the passage. Then answer the questions.

Skin
Protects Skin

We should apply sunscreen with an SPF rating of at least 15 and reapply it every two hours.

What is your body's largest organ? Yes, it is your skin. Skin is made up of three layers. Touch your skin – this outer layer that you can feel is the epidermis. Other than making new skin cells, the epidermis produces melanin, a pigment that gives your skin its colour. The next layer down is the dermis. The dermis contains blood vessels, oil glands, sweat glands, and nerve endings that work with the nervous system. The hypodermis is the bottom layer where the roots of your hair are found. It is also made of fat which regulates body temperature and keeps you warm.

Your skin knows that the sun's ultraviolet rays (UV rays) can be very harmful. Therefore, when UV rays hit, it protects itself by producing extra melanin. This extra melanin acts as a shield to prevent UV rays from damaging the deeper layers of the skin. However, if the UV rays exceed what your melanin can block, you will get a sunburn. This is why you must wear sunscreen to avoid sunburn and to prevent skin cancer.

Though UV rays can be harmful, we need sunlight for our bodies to make vitamin D for building strong bones. Do not hide from the sun; just be sure that your skin is properly protected.

ISBN: 978-1-897457-77-1

1. Label the diagram. Then write one function for each layer.

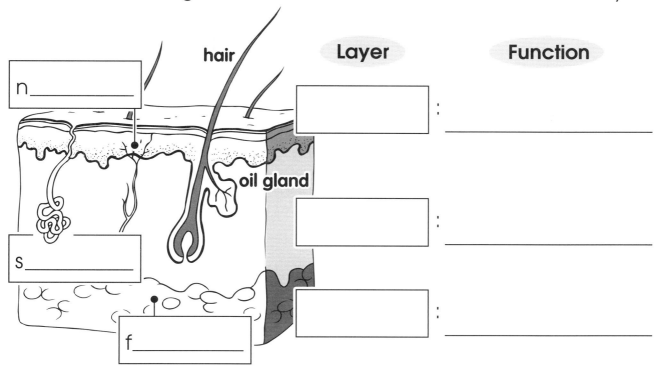

hair

Layer

Function

n_____

s_____

oil gland

f_____

_____ : _____

_____ : _____

_____ : _____

2. Complete the sentences.

How Skin Reacts to Sun Rays

first 15 min

Skin produces extra a._____ , which acts as a shield to prevent b._____ from damaging the skin.

sun rays   **first 15 min**

after 15 min

When the c._____ exceed what your d._____ can block, you will get a sunburn.

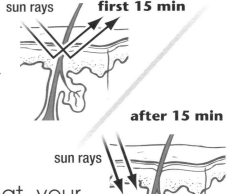

after 15 min

sun rays

3. Explain why your skin tans after you spend time under the sun.

_____

_____

Experiment

Introduction

Your heart sends blood filled with oxygen and nutrients through your arteries to all the cells in your body. When you are exercising, your muscles work harder and need more oxygen. So will your heart beat faster when you exercise?

Hypothesis

The more intense the exercise is, the faster the heart beats.

Steps

1. Sit down to get yourself rested and your breathing steady.

2.  Use your fingertips to find the pulse in your wrist.

3. Time yourself with the watch or clock and count the number of beats you feel in a minute.

4. Record your heart rate in beats per minute (bpm).

Materials

- *a watch or clock that can measure seconds*

ISBN 978-1-897457-77-1

5. Take a short walk for about 2 minutes at a park.

6. Repeat steps 2 to 4.

7. Sit down until you are rested and your breathing is steady.

8. Run for about one minute at a park.

9. Repeat steps 2 to 4.

Result

at rest

_____ bpm

after walking

_____ bpm

after running

_____ bpm

Conclusion

The hypothesis was: _____

_____

My experiment _____ the hypothesis.

supported/did not support

Try to complete this review in **30 minutes**.

30 minutes

This review consists of five sections, from A to E. The marks for each question are shown in parentheses. The circle at the bottom right corner is for the marks you get in each section. An overall record is on the last page of the review.

A. Write T for true and F for false.

1. The cerebrum is the largest part of the brain. **(2)** _____

2. A valve opens to let blood flow from the right ventricle to the right atrium. **(2)** _____

3. 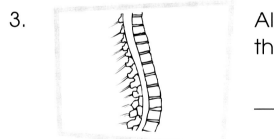 All nerves in the body are protected by the spine. **(2)**

   _____

4. 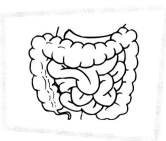 Waste is stored in the small intestine before it gets excreted. **(2)**

   _____

8

ISBN: 978-1-897457-77-1

B. Do the matching.

1.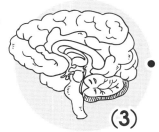
(3)

2.
(3)

3.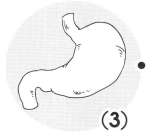
(3)

4.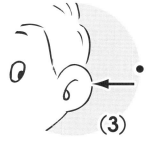
(3)

5.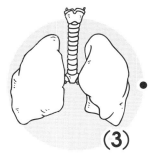
(3)

- contains cartilage

- contains gastric juice

- part of the nervous system

- helps prevent skin cancer

- the organs affected by asthma

15

ISBN: 978-1-897457-77-1

C. Name the important systems in our body. Write one of the major organs and the main function of each system.

1.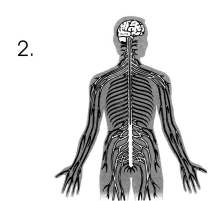

_____ system ; _____ **(2)**

main function: _____

_____

_____ **(3)**

2.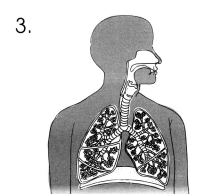

_____ system ; _____ **(2)**

main function: _____

_____

_____ **(3)**

3.

_____ system ; _____ **(2)**

main function: _____

_____

_____ **(3)**

4.

_____ system ; _____ **(2)**

main function: _____

_____

_____ **(3)**

20

ISBN 978-1-897457-77-1

D. **Label the organs and write the organs that food passes through in the digestive system. Then answer the questions.**

1.   **Digestive System**

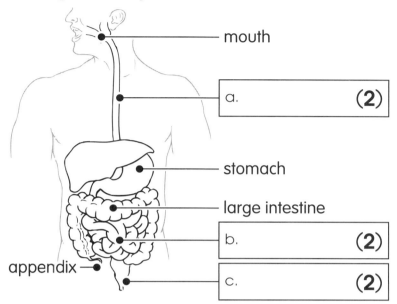

mouth

a. _____ **(2)**

stomach

large intestine

b. _____ **(2)**

c. _____ **(2)**

appendix

Food Passing through the Digestive System

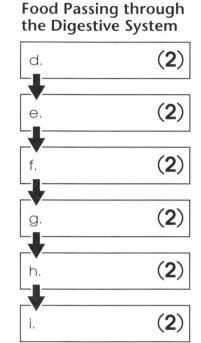

d. _____ **(2)**

e. _____ **(2)**

f. _____ **(2)**

g. _____ **(2)**

h. _____ **(2)**

i. _____ **(2)**

2.   Functions of the digestive system: **(3)**

_____

_____

3.   What is the function of a stomach? What substances help it do its job? **(4)**

_____

_____

4.   Identify each activity as an "involuntary" or a "voluntary" action. Then write the part of the brain that is responsible for controlling that activity.

   a.   jumping: _____ action;

        controlled by the _____ **(4)**

   b.   movement of the stomach: _____ action;

        controlled by the _____ **(4)**

33

ISBN: 978-1-897457-77-1

E. Look at the side view below. Name the organs. Then answer the questions.

1.

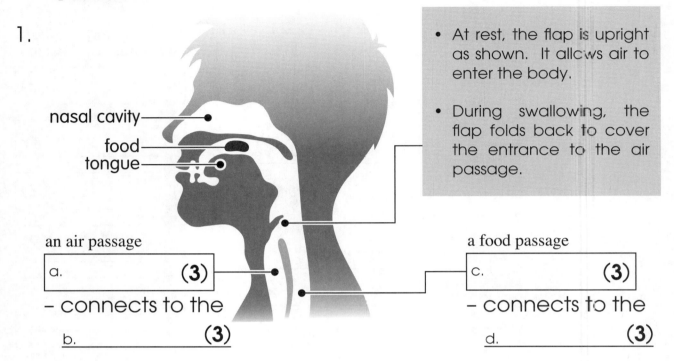

- At rest, the flap is upright as shown. It allows air to enter the body.

- During swallowing, the flap folds back to cover the entrance to the air passage.

nasal cavity
food
tongue

an air passage

a.	**(3)**

– connects to the

b. **(3)**

a food passage

c.	**(3)**

– connects to the

d. **(3)**

2. Draw arrows to show the paths. Then draw the missing flaps.

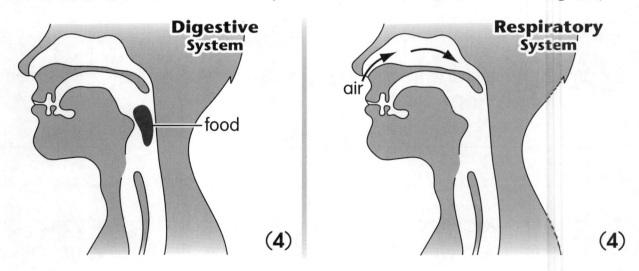

Digestive System

food

(4)

Respiratory System

air

(4)

3. Is the movement of the flap voluntary or involuntary? Which body system is responsible for this movement? **(4)**

_____

_____

24

ISBN: 978-1-897457-77-1

My Record

Section A	8
Section B	15
Section C	20
Section D	33
Section E	24

Total

100

80-100

Great work! You really understand your science stuff! Research your favourite science topics at the library or on the Internet to find out more about the topics related to this section. Keep challenging yourself to learn more!

60-79

Good work! You understand some basic concepts, but try reading through the units again to see whether you can master the material! Go over the questions that you had trouble with to make sure you know the correct answers.

below 60

You can do much better! Try reading over the units again. Ask your parents or teachers any questions you might have. Once you feel confident that you know the material, try the review again. Science is exciting, so don't give up!

ISBN: 978-1-897457-77-1

The Doctor

The human body is made up of organ systems that work together as one unit. The heart, blood vessels, and blood, for example, form the cardiovascular system. The digestive system is made up of four primary organs (mouth, stomach, intestines, and rectum) and another four accessory organs (teeth, tongue, liver, and pancreas).

When any of our organs does not function properly, we will not feel well and have to go to the doctor for treatment. Doctors are specially trained people who know a lot about organs and how they work as systems. Since the human body is very complex, it is impossible for a doctor to know all the organ systems equally well. Doctors have to specialize. Cardiologists, for example, specialize in treating disorders in the cardiovascular system. Optometrists are doctors who take care of our eyes and vision. Some disorders cannot be healed simply by taking medicine. They need surgery. Surgeons are doctors who perform surgery to treat diseases. Surgery involves removing a diseased organ or repairing a tear or breakage.

Are you interested in the human body? Do you want to become a doctor? Which organ system would you like to specialize in?

HUMAN HEART

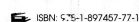 ISBN: 975-1-897457-77-1

Cool Science Facts

1 Where is your funny bone? What makes it "funny"?

2 How long does the food you ate stay in your body?

3 Why do we get goose bumps?

4 What does colour tell you about a vegetable or fruit?

5 Do we get more bones as we get older?

Find the answers on the next page.

ISBN: 978-1-897457-77-1

Cool Science Facts

1 The funny bone is actually not a bone. It is a nerve called ulnar nerve in your elbow. If you bang your elbow at a certain spot that bumps the ulnar nerve against the humerus bone, you get a tingling feeling that feels funny.

humerus

ulnar nerve

2 After you have eaten something, it takes the food approximately 8 hours to pass through the stomach to the small intestines. After that, it takes between 12 and 72 hours to digest the food, depending on what you have eaten. Red meat takes a lot longer to digest than fruit and vegetables.

after 20 to 80 hours

ISBN: 978-1-897457-77-1

4 The colour tells you about the benefits of a vegetable or fruit.

red: fight heart diseases (tomato, grapefruit)

green: reduce risks of cancer (kiwifruit, lime)

orange/yellow: boost immune system (mango, apricot)

blue/purple: lower blood pressure (blueberry, eggplant)

To maintain good health, we should fill our plates with not only green leaves but also other colourful vegetables and fruit.

5 When we were born, we had about 300 bones in the bodies. As we grow, our bones grow too, but we do not get more of them. Instead, some of them fuse together, so when we are adults, we only have 206 bones.

More Bones

3 When it is cold, the muscles attached to the base of each hair contract in order to trap the body heat to keep you warm. Hence, the ducts get smaller and tighten up. This pulls the hair up, making your skin up, making goose bumps.

David, I can see your goose bumps.

ISBN: 978-1-897457-77-1

ISBN: 973-1-897457-77-1

Section 2

Understanding
Structures and Mechanisms

ISBN: 978-1-897457-77-1

1 Effects of Natural Forces

The forces from natural occurrences affect structures in different ways. Sometimes, the forces are tremendous. In this unit, you will see how structures are affected by natural occurrences and how they are built to withstand these forces.

After completing this unit, you will

- know how natural occurrences affect structures.
- know what we can do to strengthen structures.

Sam, start with the lowest speed to see how much wind force our bridge can withstand. Then turn it up if the bridge is still holding strong.

Natural Occurrences

lightning

wind

rain

v o c a b u l a r y

natural occurrence: event caused by nature and not by humans

Extension

The effects of natural erosion on human-made structures can be hard to see over the course of a day or even a year. Only when we observe how a structure changes over hundreds or thousands of years can we see erosion's slow but significant impact. The Great Pyramid of Giza was 146 m tall when it was built, but over 4500 years, this height has decreased to a current height of 139 m. Scientists believe that erosion by natural occurrences has contributed to this reduction of height.

How tall would it be after another 4500 years?

146 m

139 m

4500 years ago

Now

After 4500 years

A. **Draw lines to show whether the forces acting on the structures are from natural occurrences or human activities.**

Forces from

Natural Occurrences •

Human Activities •

- ocean waves damaging a sandcastle

- heavy rain flooding a house

- an overload collapsing a bridge

- an earthquake cracking a wall

ISBN: 978-1-897457-77-1

B. **Identify the natural occurrences. Fill in the blanks to show the effects of natural occurrences on structures.**

Impacts on Structures from Natural Occurrences

tsunami   flood   tornado

hurricane   snowstorm   earthquake

rain   wind   waves   snow   surface   wind

1. _____ : has intense _____ speed that can lift up buildings and toss vehicles over long distances

2. _____ : shakes the earth's _____ ; weakens the framework of a structure, causing it to collapse

3. _____ : accumulated _____ on roofs causes them to collapse

4. _____ : strong ocean _____ run over the land, destroying or damaging structures

5. _____ : heavy _____ accumulates on land causing damage to structures

6. _____ : consists of heavy rain that causes floods and _____ that lifts up roofs

    ISBN: 978-1-897457-77-1

C. Fill in the blanks to show what techniques are used to build safer buildings.

Building Safer Buildings

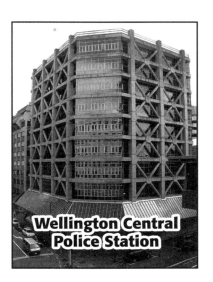

brick	flexible
crisscrossing	steel

1. Protecting from Earthquakes

- Use a._____ materials, so they bend rather than break under impact. b._____ is not an ideal material in this case.

- Buildings can be built with a c._____ frame.

- Walls can be reinforced with diagonal d._____ bars.

Wellington Central Police Station

2. Protecting from Floods/Hurricanes

higher	masts
drainage	masts curved

- Install a foundation a._____ system.

- Put foundation deep in the ground to avoid erosion of the b._____ and make the corners c._____ to reduce the impact of strong winds and water.

- Buildings can be built on d._____ ground or on steel e._____ so that they are lifted off the ground.

3. Protecting from High Winds

shutters slope roof
in   water

- Install a._____ on the windows.

- Have doors open b._____ rather than out.

- Tie the c._____ to the walls to prevent it from being blown off.

- Build a roof with a gentle d._____ to reduce the impact of the wind and help drain the e._____ off the roof.

D. Read the passage. Then answer the questions.

The House
that Zadie's Dad Will Build

As Zadie's dad draws plans for the house he will build, she asks him to explain the plan. "This is the **foundation**," he says to her, pointing to the house's base. "It separates the house from the ground. It will be the first thing I build."

"Next, I'll build the floor: **beams** will run the length of the house, and **joists** will run between the beams across the width of the house. The walls will be next; they'll be made of **studs**, the vertical supports for the house. I'll build the ceiling with beams, and I'll use **trusses** to build the roof."

"Dad, what are trusses?"

"Trusses are triangles with structural supports within them. I'll buy them already made. Some builders build simple triangles from two pieces of wood that join at the roof's peak, called **rafters**, and another at the base, called a **joist**. At their peak, the trusses are held in place by a **beam** that runs the length of the house."

"Then the frame will be finished," Zadie says happily.

"Yes, it will," her dad says, smiling.

ISBN: 978-1-897457-77-1

1. Label the parts of the house.

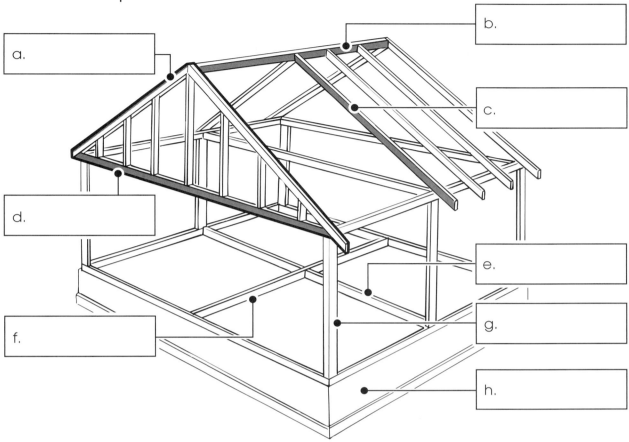

a.

b.

c.

d.

e.

f.

g.

h.

2. How does the triangular roof benefit the house?

_____

_____

3. Check the truss below that has a better design than the one above. Explain your choice.

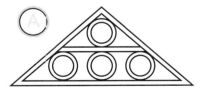
(A)

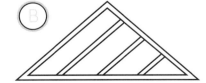
(B)

(C)

Explain: _____

_____

ISBN: 978-1-897457-77-1

2 Impacts on Structures

All around us are structures. In this unit, you will be focusing on how society and the environment impact structures. You will also learn about ways people find to minimize the disruption a structure has on society and the environment.

After completing this unit, you will

- understand how society and the environment impact structures.

- know how to minimize impacts on structures by using suitable tools and techniques.

Stop running! The whole house is shaking!

Vocabulary

unfrozen soil

permafrost

unfrozen ground

permafrost: soil that remains frozen for two or more years

ISBN: 978-1-897457-77-1

Have you ever seen the Leaning Tower of Pisa? When engineers built the tower, they knew that they were building on a thick layer of wet sandy soil, covered by a thin layer of clay. For this reason, they built a few levels first and let them settle on the soft ground before progressing. When they decided to continue with the construction, they thought that the tower had already settled, but in fact, it started to lean to one side due to the unstable ground. To this day, engineers find ways to reinforce the foundation and stabilize the tower while keeping it tilted.

Next time you go to the beach, bring a big bottle of bubble soap. Wet some sand and stand the bottle up in the sand. You can see that the bottle tilts just like the Leaning Tower.

A. Pair up the ground materials and the structures that they would support. Write the answers on the lines.

Ground Materials: Structures that Are Supported

1. _____ : _____
   composed of cement

2. _____ : _____
   grows on lawns

3. _____ : _____
   tiny pieces of rock

4. _____ : _____
   loose rocks

5. _____ : _____
   solid form of water

Materials

grass
concrete
ice
sand
gravel

Structures

igloo
skyscraper
tent
sandcastle
playground

B. Read the story and analyze the problem. Circle the correct answers.

A few years ago, a hotel was built in the Yukon. Recently, the frozen ground under the hotel has started to thaw. This incident poses a serious problem to the structure.

1. **Cause of the Problem**

   • The **heat / smoke** that is given off from the hotel can thaw the permafrost underneath the hotel.

   • When the melted permafrost under the hotel refreezes, it **evaporates / expands**, causing the hotel to **lift up from / sink into** the ground.

2. **Problems**

   • When the ground thaws, the **foundation / lighting** of the hotel begins to shift, damaging its structure.

   • The floor of the hotel becomes **smooth / uneven** and creaky.

   • **Cracks / Crystals** form in the walls and ceilings.

   • Building materials are affected by the prolonged exposure to **air / water** .

ISBN: 978-1-897457-77-1

3. **Solutions**

- Use **pillars / baskets** to keep the hot water pipes up off the ground to avoid heating the frozen ground.

- Add crushed **ice / rocks** around the footings of the hotel to insulate the ground and stabilize the foundation.

- **Insulate / Open** the foundation walls and floors to trap the heat inside and prevent direct contact with the ground.

4. If none of the solutions are implemented, what will happen to the hotel?

_____

5. Skyscrapers are tall buildings and they need deep foundations. Do you think it is a good idea to build a skyscraper in the Yukon? Explain.

_____

_____

6. Some sharp bumps are found on the road outside the hotel, making it unsafe for driving.

   a. What has happened to the road? Explain.

   _____
   _____

   b. Check the better solution.

   (A) Replace the soil under the road with gravel to insulate the permafrost.

   (B) Build another road to replace the existing one.

C. **Read Zadie's notes. Then number the steps and answer the questions.**

Zadie's Dad Builds a Foundation

Zadie goes with her dad to the building site and takes notes on what she sees:

July 1

Dad is about to build the crawl space, a kind of foundation. He says crawl spaces keep the house's wooden frame off the ground so that it doesn't get wet, and they make it easy to repair the heating, plumbing, and electrical systems because workers can get underneath the house.

First, Dad and his friends dig a hole with a machine. Around the hole, they dig a trench. They frame the trench with wooden boards, and pour concrete between the boards. They wait for the concrete to set.

July 16

Dad removes the wooden boards and begins building walls on the concrete base using cinder blocks. Dad tells me he will build the walls until they are above the ground.

July 19

The walls are finished. Dad and his friends insulate the walls with foam pads. They fill the top layer of cinder blocks with concrete and stick metal rods called anchor bolts into the concrete. The anchor bolts will hold the wooden frame in place when they begin to build the house. So, now the foundation is done!

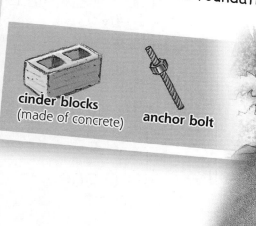

cinder blocks
(made of concrete)   anchor bolt

ISBN 978-1-897457-77-1

1.

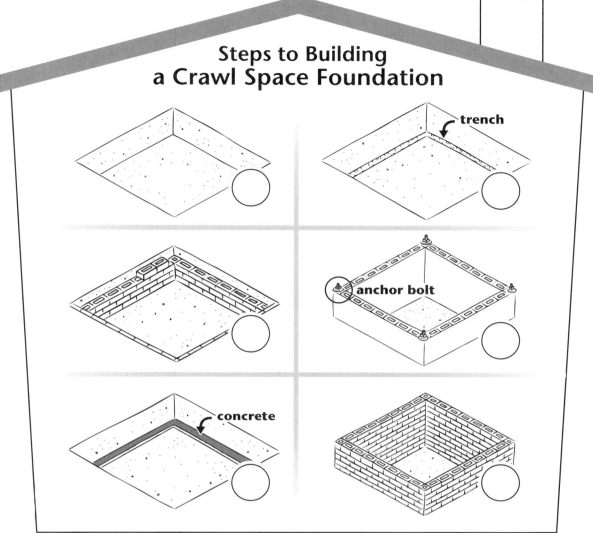

Steps to Building a Crawl Space Foundation

trench

anchor bolt

concrete

2. What is the purpose of a crawl space foundation?

_____

_____

3. What material plays an important role in building foundations? What properties does this material have to make it reliable?

_____

_____

3 External and Internal Forces

Any force can either be an external or an internal force. In this unit, you will distinguish between these two forces and identify their different types.

After completing this unit, you will

- know what external and internal forces are.
- be able to identify different types of external and internal forces.
- understand how compression and tension act on structures.

greater internal force

My bowl can withstand the external force because it has a greater internal force than yours.

Vocabulary

compression: a pushing force

tension: a pulling force

torsion: a turning or twisting force

bending: a force that compresses one side of an object and stretches the other side

Types of Internal Forces

compression   **tension**   **torsion**

bending

ISBN 978-1-897457-77-1

Have you ever played with a paddle ball – a toy with a ball attached to a paddle by an elastic string? Every time the ball is hit, it becomes a load and puts tension on the string. However, since the string is elastic, it has the tendency to return to its original length. Therefore, after the elastic string is pulled, it will reinstate itself by pulling the ball back towards the paddle with its compression force.

Consider the adventurous and challenging game, bungee jumping. How does the elastic rope attached to a jumper allow the jumper to feel excitement from falling but also be kept safe from the drop?

A. Fill in the boxes with "external" or "internal". Then fill in the blanks for each picture.

1.

Force

a. _____ force:
the force that acts on a structure from the outside

b. _____ force:
the force that acts from within the structure

2.

- The wind is an a._____ force and the trees keep themselves from falling over with their b._____ forces.

- The hands are the c._____ force bending the ruler, while the ruler's d._____ force keeps it from breaking.

B. There are two types of external forces. Fill in the boxes with "live load" or "dead load". Then state the types of external forces in each picture and explain your choice.

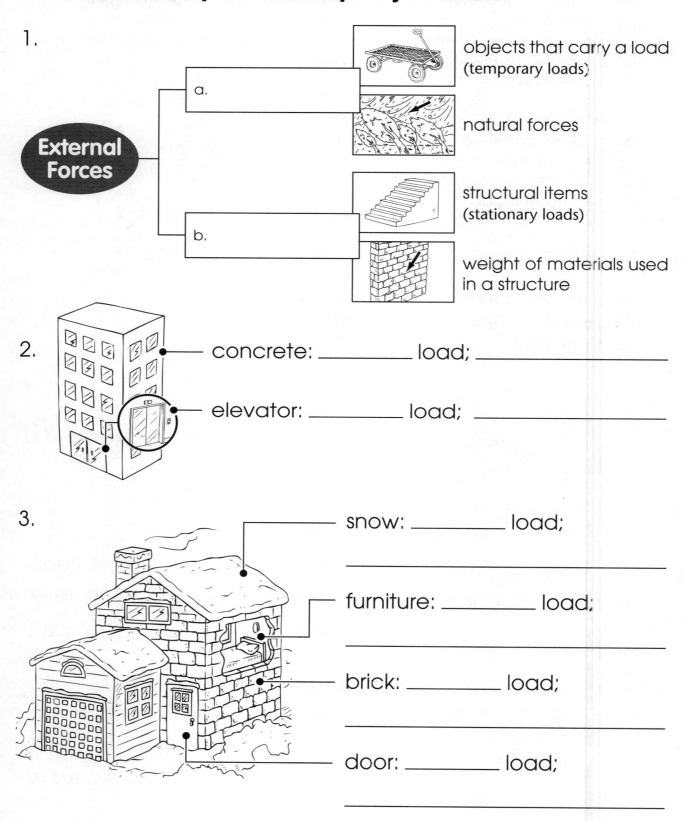

1.

a.

b.

External Forces

objects that carry a load (temporary loads)

natural forces

structural items (stationary loads)

weight of materials used in a structure

2. concrete: _____ load; _____

elevator: _____ load; _____

3. snow: _____ load;

_____

furniture: _____ load;

_____

brick: _____ load;

_____

door: _____ load;

_____

ISBN: 978-1-897457-77-1

C. Draw a line to match each internal force with its meaning. Then identify the internal forces shown in the pictures.

1.

Internal Forces

compression •

tension •

torsion •

bending •

• a turning force

• a pushing force

• a pulling force

• a force that causes compression on one side and tension on the other

2.

a.

b.

c.

d.

e.

f.

3.

_____

4.

_____

5.

_____

6.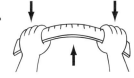

_____

D. Read Jack's science assignment. Then answer the questions.

Mr. McGrath's Grade 5 Science Assignment   Name: _Jack_

Objective: To design a strong and stable bookcase with 2 shelves that will hold at least 10 thick books and 10 thin books

Assignment: Decide on your design by answering the questions below. Then draw diagrams to show your work.

All about the Bookcase:

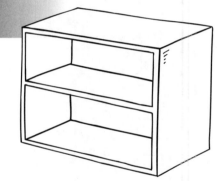

1. Material (explain your choice):

    foam blocks / wood / bricks

2. State the live and dead loads.

3. Which part of the bookcase is under compression and which is in tension? Which parts of the bookcase show bending forces?

4. Add brackets to support the shelf. What force will act on the brackets?

bracket

5. How should the books be put on the bookcase to help the structure be more stable?*

* Think about the centre of gravity, which is the point where the total mass of an object is concentrated.

ISBN: 978-1-897457-77-1

1. Material used:

_____

_____

_____

2. Live load: _____

   Dead load: _____

3 & 4. Parts under compression, parts in tension, and parts that show bending forces:

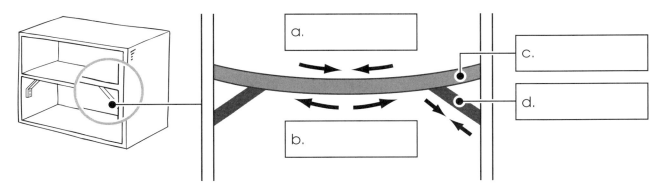

a. _____

b. _____

c. _____

d. _____

When the books are put on the shelf, one side of the shelf is

under compression and the other side is in e._____ .

This creates a f._____ force on the shelf.

5.

_____

_____

_____

_____

Introduction

Architects and scientists work together to find materials that are strong, inexpensive, and can be easily assembled for making bridges' piers. If the material used for each pier is doubled or even tripled, how much more load can the structure support?

Hypothesis

A structure supports _____ times more load if the material used in a pier is tripled.

Steps

1. Build a cube by attaching the pieces of spaghetti to the marshmallows.

Materials

- **32 pieces of uncooked spaghetti**
- **16 large marshmallows**
- **rolls of toilet paper**
- **a piece of cardboard**

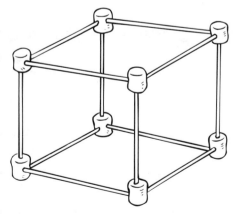

2. Put a piece of cardboard on the structure.

3. Place rolls of toilet paper on the cardboard until the structure collapses.

4. Record the number of rolls the structure can hold.

5. Build a cube the same way as the previous one, but have each vertical support be made of 3 pieces of spaghetti.

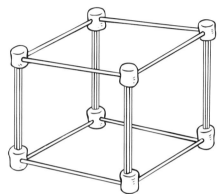

6. Repeat steps 2 to 4.

Result

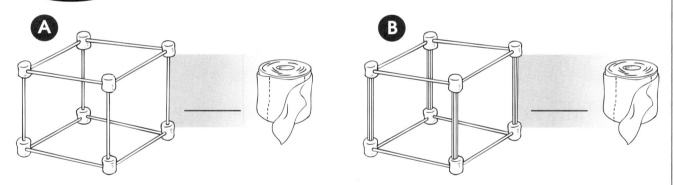

A _____

B _____

Structure **B** supported _____ times more load.

Conclusion

The hypothesis was: _____

_____

My experiment _____ the hypothesis.

supported/did not support

4 Bridges and Forces

The stability and strength of a bridge depends on its ability to distribute the weight of a load. In this unit, you will explore different types of bridges and how forces act on them.

After completing this unit, you will

- be able to identify different types of bridges.
- understand how forces act on different bridges.

an arch bridge

Look! I can build the strongest bridge in the world.

Vocabulary

cantilever: a beam that is kept in balance by a counterweight

counterweight: a weight that balances a load

counterweight

The Québec Bridge is one of Canada's most famous structures because it is the longest cantilever bridge in the world. A cantilever bridge consists of two cantilever arms. Each cantilever arm has one end anchored onto a supporter while the other end is suspended. To create a span, the suspended ends of the cantilever arms are placed end to end, meeting at the centre; to make the bridge longer, a short span can be added in between. To counterbalance the weight of the cantilever arms, the end of each cantilever arm is anchored with a counterweight, called anchor arm.

Imagine your friend and yourself on a see-saw. Think about how your friend counterbalances your weight.

short span

Québec Bridge

supporter

A. Name the bridges. Then match them with the correct descriptions.

arch bridge	**A**	has a beam hung from cables
truss bridge	**B**	has an arch to transfer the load to the supporters
suspension bridge	**C**	has a simple beam to support a load crossing a gap
beam bridge	**D**	has a beam composed of connected steel triangles

1.

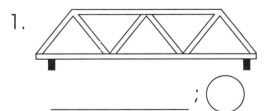

_____ ; ◯

2.

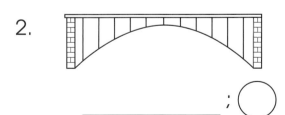

_____ ; ◯

3.

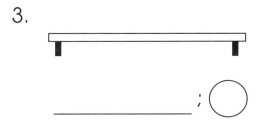

_____ ; ◯

4.

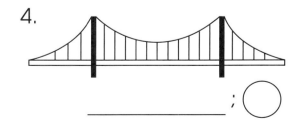

_____ ; ◯

ISBN: 978-1-897457-77-1

B. Name the bridges. Identify each "live load" and "dead load" acting on the bridges. Colour the arrows to show how compression and tension work. Then answer the question.

1.

> A bridge must be strong enough to support its own weight and the weight of the vehicles crossing it. It also needs reinforcement to withstand natural forces.

compression: red   tension: blue

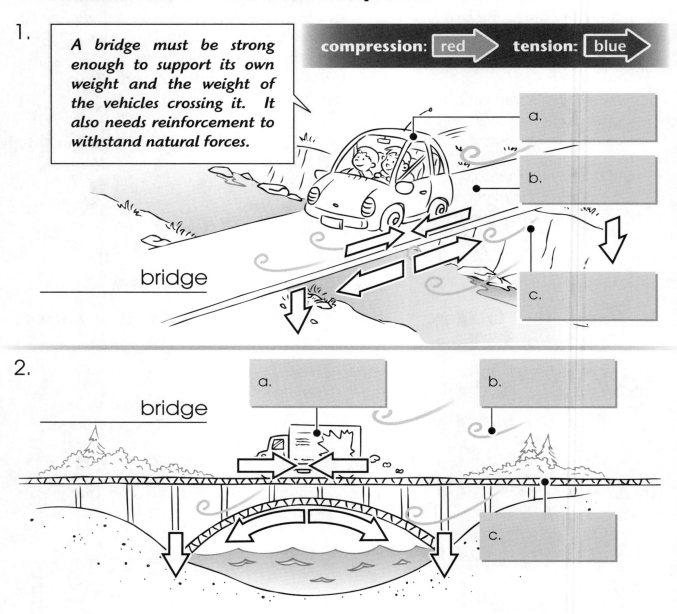

_____ bridge

a.

b.

c.

2.

_____ bridge

a.   b.

c.

3. Check the correct circles to show what we should consider when we build a bridge.

(A) weight of the bridge   (B) amount of sunshine

(C) weight of the load   (D) natural forces

(E) distance the bridge   (F) number of people who
     spans   will like the bridge

C. Name the bridges and the parts of the bridges. Colour the parts to show the compression and tension on the bridges. Then fill in the blanks.

suspension truss	truss cable suspender tower	compression: red tension: blue

1. a. _____ bridge

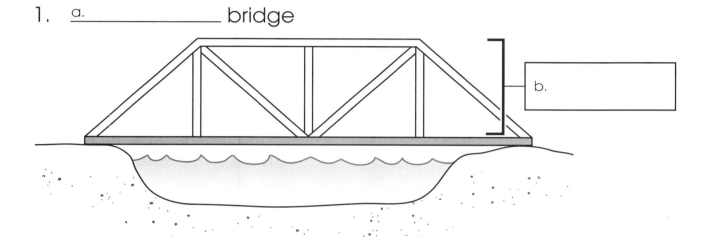

b. _____

2. a. _____ bridge

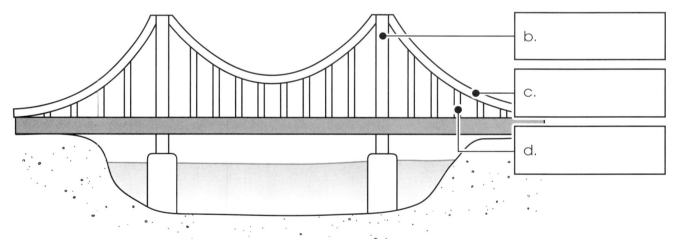

b. _____

c. _____

d. _____

3. There is a _____ force acting on the deck of the bridge. The top side of the deck is under _____ and the bottom is in _____ .

compression
bending
tension

D. Read the passage. Then answer the questions.

When a bridge spans a river, its pillars must be sturdy enough to support its weight and load; hence, concrete is a perfect material to use. Furthermore, these pillars must stand on the bedrock because it makes a sturdy foundation for bridges. However, bedrock lies below the riverbed, and before concrete can be poured onto the bedrock, the riverbed sediment must be dug out. How can this be done underwater? The first thing is to create an environment that has no water in it. To do so, bridge builders use caissons, which are huge tubes or boxes with no bottoms. By pushing a caisson straight down into the water, no water can get into the caisson. The caisson gets pushed down until its bottom rests on the riverbed while the top stays above the water's surface. After the caisson is settled, riverbed sediment inside the caisson gets dug out until the bedrock is reached.

Caisson —
Where Bridges Stand

Then, concrete in liquid form is poured into the caisson which now acts as a mould to give the concrete its pillar shape. Within weeks, the concrete hardens and is strong enough to support a bridge.

No water can get inside the bucket if I push it straight down.

ISBN: 978-1-897457-77-1

1. Follow the diagrams to write the steps to making a pillar.

Steps to Making a Pillar

riverbed sediment

bedrock

1 _____

_____

2 _____

_____

3 _____

_____

4 _____

_____

2. Check the properties of concrete that make it a suitable material for building pillars.

(A) sturdy   (B) low malleability

(C) soft   (D) corrosion resistant

(E) low elasticity (F) water resistant

5 Mechanical Systems

Simple machines help make our work easier and faster. A series of simple machines can form a mechanical system that helps us do work in an even more efficient way. In this unit, we will investigate how simple machines work together to make mechanical systems and how these systems give us advantages.

After completing this unit, you will

- be able to identify the simple machines.

- understand how mechanical systems provide mechanical advantages.

- know the three classes of levers.

> *See how smart I am for using a longer plank to gain mechanical advantage. This makes my work much easier.*

10 m

5 m

5 m

15 m

$$MA^* = \frac{10\ m}{5\ m}$$
$$= 2$$

$$MA^* = \frac{15\ m}{5\ m}$$
$$= 3$$

* **MA: mechanical advantage**

vocabulary

> *I can move the box with only 20 N.*

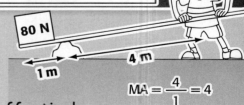

80 N

1 m

4 m

$$MA = \frac{4}{1} = 4$$

mechanical system: a system that uses one or more simple machines

mechanical advantage: a measure to describe how effectively a simple machine works

ISBN: 978-1-897457-77-1

We use simple machines to help us do complex and heavy tasks. Rube Goldberg, a famous artist, was different; he "invented" complex machines to do simple tasks. He created machines using gears, levers, pails, and anything he could think of. Some of his most popular "inventions" include: Self-Operating Napkin, Simple Alarm Clock, and Simplified Pencil Sharpener.

Can you describe how this machine works? What does it do?

A. Identify the six simple machines. Then give an example of a common tool containing each.

1. _____ : e.g. _____
   a flat slanted surface

   wedge

2. _____ : e.g. _____
   used with a fulcrum

   lever

3. _____ : e.g. _____
   a wheel attached to an axle

   wheel and axle

4. _____ : e.g. _____
   a wheel with a rope wrapped around it

   pulley

5. _____ : e.g. _____
   a shaft with a spiral-shaped groove on its surface

   screw

6. _____ : e.g. _____
   a back-to-back inclined plane; may hold things together or pull them apart

   inclined plane

B. **Use the formula to calculate the mechanical advantage of each machine and the force needed to move the load.**

1. **Mechanical Advantage of a Lever / an Inclined Plane**
   (how much the machine magnifies effort)

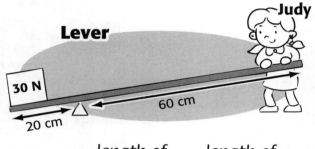

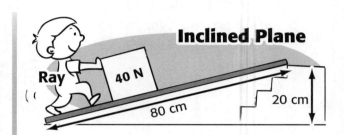

$$MA = \frac{\text{length of effort arm}}{} \div \frac{\text{length of load arm}}{}$$

= _____ ÷ _____

= _____

The lever magnifies the effort _____ times. Judy needs _____ N of force to move the load.

$$MA = \text{its length} \div \text{its height}$$

= _____ ÷ _____

= _____

The inclined plane magnifies the effort _____ times. Ray needs _____ N of force to move the load.

2.

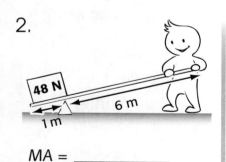

MA = _____

Force needed : _____

3.

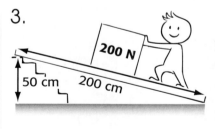

MA = _____

Force needed : _____

4.

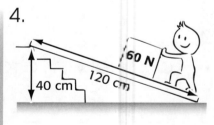

MA = _____

Force needed : _____

5. The greater the MA is, the _____ force is needed to move a load.
   less/more

ISBN: 978-1-897457-77-1

C. Colour the supporting ropes. Find the mechanical advantage of each pulley system and the force needed to move the load. Then answer the questions.

The mechanical advantage of a pulley is equal to the number of supporting ropes. The amount of force needed to move the load can be found by dividing the weight of the load by the MA.

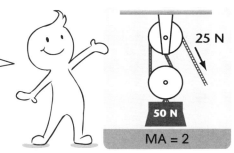

25 N

50 N

MA = 2

1.

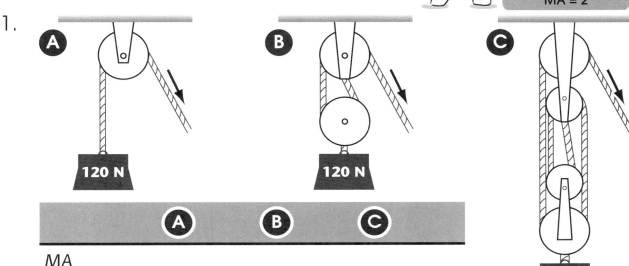

A   120 N

B   120 N

C   120 N

	A	B	C
MA			
Force			

2. Which pulley system needs the least force to move the load? _____

3. The greater the MA is, the _____ force is needed to move a load.
   less/more

4. What is the disadvantage of using pulley **B** or **C** to move the load?

   Ⓐ It has less mechanical advantage than using one pulley.

   Ⓑ A person cannot use his or her body weight to move the load.

   Ⓒ The effort needs to travel a longer distance than it would with one pulley.

D. Read about the three classes of levers. Then answer the questions.

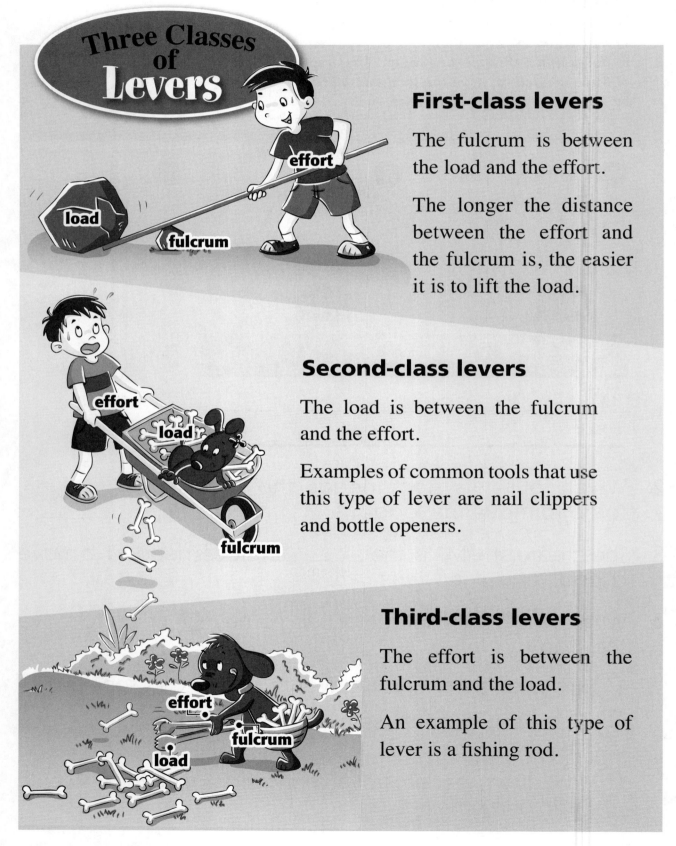

Three Classes of Levers

First-class levers

The fulcrum is between the load and the effort.

The longer the distance between the effort and the fulcrum is, the easier it is to lift the load.

Second-class levers

The load is between the fulcrum and the effort.

Examples of common tools that use this type of lever are nail clippers and bottle openers.

Third-class levers

The effort is between the fulcrum and the load.

An example of this type of lever is a fishing rod.

ISBN 978-1-897457-77-1

1. Label the parts of each diagram as "effort", "load", or "fulcrum". Identify the class of lever each diagram shows. Then give three examples of each.

a. _____ - class lever

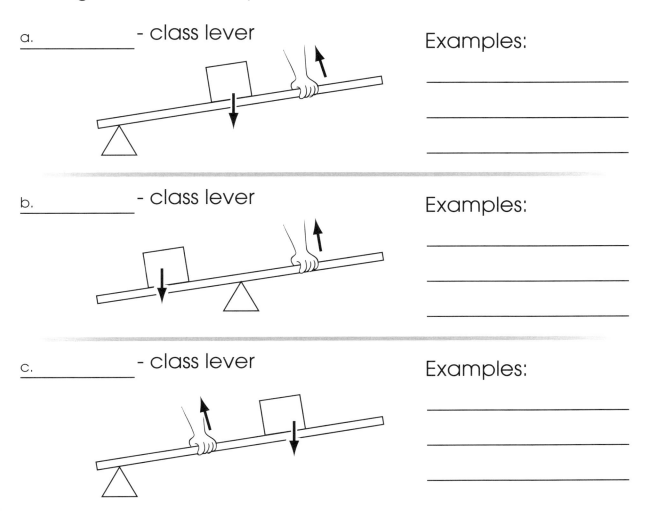

Examples:

_____
_____
_____

b. _____ - class lever

Examples:

_____
_____
_____

c. _____ - class lever

Examples:

_____
_____
_____

2. Which simple machine combines with a lever to form each compound machine below? Name the simple machine and the class of the lever.

	simple machine	lever
A	_____ +	_____
B	_____ +	_____

6 Protective Equipment

Our bodies are subject to the impact of various forces. In order to protect our bodies during certain activities, it is important to wear protective equipment. In this unit, you will look at the different protective equipment used in sports and by safety workers.

After completing this unit, you will

- know what protective equipment should be worn by sports players and safety workers.
- know how different equipment serves different purposes.

Julie, you're wearing the wrong helmet. We must always wear the right equipment to protect our bodies.

Protective Equipment

helmet

goggles

Vocabulary

protective equipment: clothing and accessories that safeguard a person's body from impact and injury

ISBN: 978-1-897457-77-1

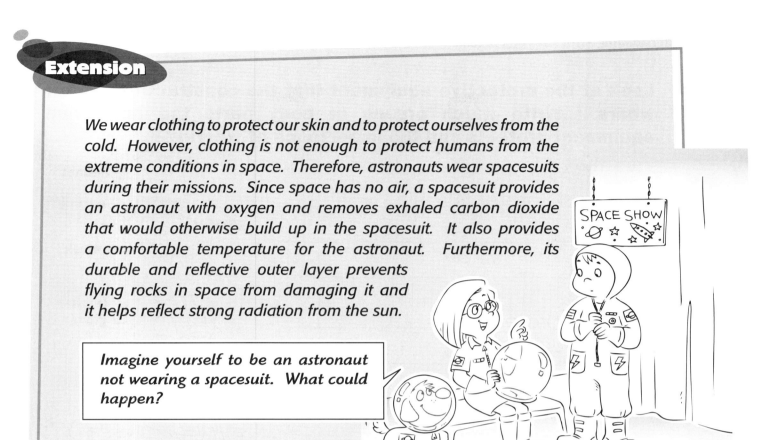

We wear clothing to protect our skin and to protect ourselves from the cold. However, clothing is not enough to protect humans from the extreme conditions in space. Therefore, astronauts wear spacesuits during their missions. Since space has no air, a spacesuit provides an astronaut with oxygen and removes exhaled carbon dioxide that would otherwise build up in the spacesuit. It also provides a comfortable temperature for the astronaut. Furthermore, its durable and reflective outer layer prevents flying rocks in space from damaging it and it helps reflect strong radiation from the sun.

Imagine yourself to be an astronaut not wearing a spacesuit. What could happen?

A. Choose the protective equipment that each sports player needs.

elbow guards   knee pads   snowsuit   rib pad
shoulder pads   helmet   wrist guards

1.
football player

2.
snowboarder

3.
inline skater

B. **Look at the protective equipment that the construction worker wears. Write which organs or body parts the protective equipment protects and the importance of wearing it.**

1. dust mask: protects _____

   _____

   _____

2. goggles: protect _____

   _____

3. earmuffs: protect _____

   _____

   _____

4. leather gloves: protect _____

   _____

5. steel-toe boots: protect _____

   _____

6. helmet: protects _____

   _____

7. Describe how the helmet of a miner is different from the one of a construction worker. Explain how this difference benefits a miner.

   _____

   _____

ISBN: 978-1-897457-77-1

C. Help each worker find the appropriate protective equipment. Write the answer on the line. Then explain your choice.

1. miner: _____

    sewage worker: _____

    _____

    _____

    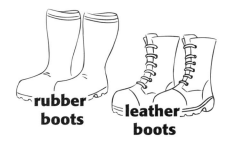
    rubber boots **leather boots**

2. chemist: _____

    welder: _____

    _____

    _____

    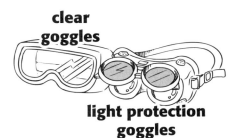
    clear goggles

    light protection goggles

3. nurse: _____

    gardener: _____

    _____

    _____

    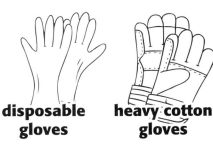
    disposable gloves **heavy cotton gloves**

4. construction worker: _____

    cyclist: _____

    _____

    _____

    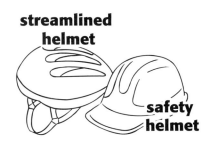
    streamlined helmet

    safety helmet

D. Read the passage. Then answer the questions.

Protective Gear for Every Part of the Body

In hockey, pucks fly, sticks are raised, players check each other, and skates cut. As a result, there is protective equipment for every part of a player's body. Perhaps the most important piece of protective equipment is the helmet, which protects a player's head and ears. Helmets are made of polycarbonate material, which is essentially lightweight plastic, and lined with a thick layer of foam padding. Attached to many helmets is a face mask, which is either a metal cage or a plastic shield. Hard plastic and foam padding shoulder pads protect the shoulders, upper back, collar bones, and ribs. Hockey gloves are made of leather and nylon, protecting the player's hands and wrists. Nylon and foam hockey pants protect a player's spine, kidneys, tailbone, and thighs. Below the hockey pants, hard plastic and foam shin pads extend to the skates to protect the lower legs. Skates are made of plastic, leather, and nylon. They protect the player, too. The inner boots keep feet comfortable, and the outer boots support the ankle and protect against sticks and pucks.

ISBN: 978-1-897457-77-1

1. Name the equipment and the materials used to make it. Then write the parts of the body that equipment protects.

Ⓐ _____ (_____) ;

protects _____

Ⓑ _____ (_____) ;

protects _____

Ⓒ _____ (_____) ;

protect _____

Ⓓ _____ (_____) ;

protect _____

Ⓔ _____ (_____) ; protect _____

_____

Ⓕ _____ (_____) ; protect _____

Ⓖ _____ (_____) ; protect _____

2. How does a helmet protect the player's head?

_____

3. Can we substitute a hockey player's helmet with a bicycle helmet? Explain.

_____

_____

Experiment

Introduction

> Protective equipment must be carefully designed so that it does its job of protecting the wearer. The materials used and the way the equipment is assembled are factors that we should consider when we design safety equipment. How does assembly affect the degree of protection?

Hypothesis

Differences in the way protective equipment is assembled change / do not change the degree of protection.

Materials

- **2 raw eggs**
- **4 small see-through plastic containers, such as pudding cups, apple sauce cups, fruit cups, and plastic eggs**
- **newspaper**
- **masking tape**

Steps

1. Put one egg into a plastic container and cover it with another one. Then seal the containers with tape.

2. Wrap the containers with the newspaper. Then put the tape around the newspaper and set it aside.

ISBN 978-1-897457-77-1

3. Put some crumpled newspaper inside the bottom of the other two containers. Fit the egg into the containers. Then seal the containers with tape.

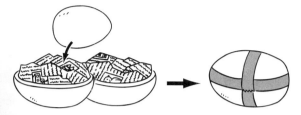

4. Drop the eggs at different levels starting with your knee level. Check the eggs to see if they break. If they are not broken, reassemble and test them at the next level. Keep testing until one of the eggs breaks.

(Write "broke" or "did not break".)

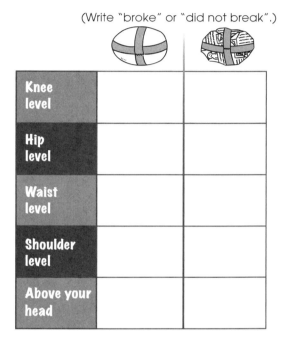

Knee level		
Hip level		
Waist level		
Shoulder level		
Above your head		

Result

Which assembly of materials better protected its egg?

_____

Conclusion

The hypothesis was: _____

_____

My experiment _____ the
hypothesis.   supported/did not support

Try to complete this review in **30 minutes**.

30 minutes

This review consists of five sections, from A to E. The marks for each question are shown in parentheses. The circle at the bottom right corner is for the marks you get in each section. An overall record is on the last page of the review.

A. Write T for true and F for false.

1. The greater the mechanical advantage is, the greater is the force needed to move a load. **(2)** _____

2. A tornado is a strong external force that acts on structures. **(2)** _____

3.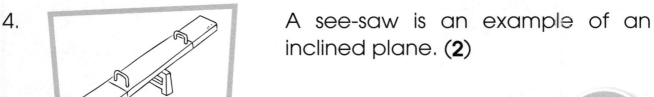

   The top side of the bridge's deck is in tension. **(2)**

   _____

4.

   A see-saw is an example of an inclined plane. **(2)**

   _____

8

ISBN: 978-1-897457-77-1

B. Do the matching.

1.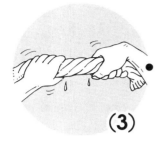

(3)

2.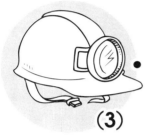

(3)

- a bridge supporter

- an example of a lever

3.

(3)

- an example of torsion force

- protective equipment for a miner

4.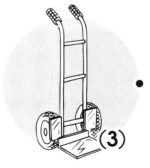

(3)

- allows rain and snow to run off

5.

(3)

15

ISBN: 978-1-897457-77-1

C. **Identify the different types of bridges. Write the letters. Then answer the questions.**

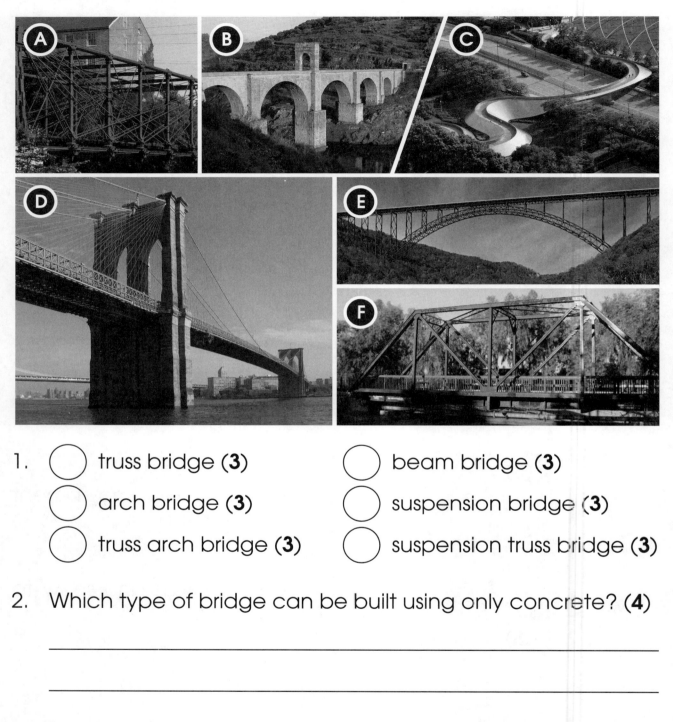

1.
- ⃝ truss bridge (**3**)
- ⃝ arch bridge (**3**)
- ⃝ truss arch bridge (**3**)
- ⃝ beam bridge (**3**)
- ⃝ suspension bridge (**3**)
- ⃝ suspension truss bridge (**3**)

2. Which type of bridge can be built using only concrete? (**4**)

_____

_____

3. Name one live load and one dead load acting on a bridge.

live load: _____ (**3**)

dead load: _____ (**3**)

28

ISBN: 978-1-897457-77-1

D. Identify each as a "live load" or "dead load" in the diagram. Then circle the correct answers and answer the questions.

1.

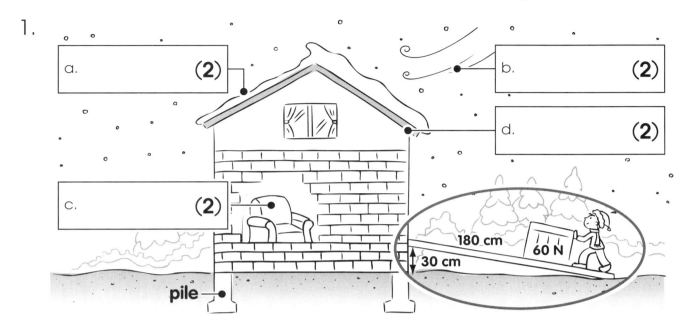

2. The best ground material for the house: **(2)**

   gravel / ice / grass / concrete

3. The force that acts on the piles: **(3)**

   tension / compression / bending force / torsion

4. A painting will be hung on a wall in the bedroom. Will the painting become a dead load or a live load of the house? **(3)**

   _____

5. What is the simple machine shown in the circle? **(3)**

   _____

6. Find the mechanical advantage of the simple machine and the force needed to move the box. **(6)**

   MA : _____   Force needed : _____

ISBN: 978-1-897457-77-1

E. Look at the picture and answer the questions.

1. Name the simple machine shown in the picture. (**2**)

    _____

2. How many supporting ropes are there to support the bucket? (**3**)

    _____

3. How much force is needed to move the bucket up? (**3**)

    _____

4.
How many supporting ropes and pulleys will there be if we want to reduce the force needed to move the bucket by half?

    _____ (**4**)

5. Which three items of protective equipment should a construction worker wear? Explain why it is important to wear each one.

    Protective Equipment for Construction Workers

    leather gloves
    wrist guards
    steel-toe boots
    snowsuit
    helmet

    a. _____ (**2**);

        importance: _____ (**2**)

    b. _____ (**2**);

        importance: _____ (**2**)

    c. _____ (**2**);

        importance: _____ (**2**)

24

ISBN: 978-1-897457-77-1

My Record

Section A	8
Section B	15
Section C	28
Section D	25
Section E	24

Total

100

80-100

Great work! You really understand your science stuff! Research your favourite science topics at the library or on the Internet to find out more about the topics related to this section. Keep challenging yourself to learn more!

60-79

Good work! You understand some basic concepts, but try reading through the units again to see whether you can master the material! Go over the questions that you had trouble with to make sure you know the correct answers.

below 60

You can do much better! Try reading over the units again. Ask your parents or teachers any questions you might have. Once you feel confident that you know the material, try the review again. Science is exciting, so don't give up!

The Architect

Have you ever wondered how some amazing buildings, bridges, and structures were built? Credits have to go to the architects who designed them. Architects are scientists who are trained to plan, design, and oversee the construction of buildings, bridges, and structures. They have to ensure that what they build is not simply beautiful and spectacular, but also practical, safe, and sturdy. To be able to achieve that, architects need to have expert knowledge of how forces act on structures and mechanisms.

The Confederation Bridge is a perfect example of the expert knowledge of architects. The bridge joins the eastern Canadian provinces of Prince Edward Island and New Brunswick, making travel easy and convenient. The curved, 12.9-kilometre-long bridge is the longest in the world crossing ice-covered water, and is considered one of Canada's top engineering achievements of the 20th century. Extremely durable high-grade concrete and reinforcing steel had to be used for the bridge because it has to withstand the forces of the ice floes during the spring thaw every year.

The architects' meticulous planning and calculations ensure that the Confederation Bridge is safe and sturdy. In fact, the lifespan of the bridge is estimated to be in excess of 100 years!

ISBN 978-1-897457-77-1

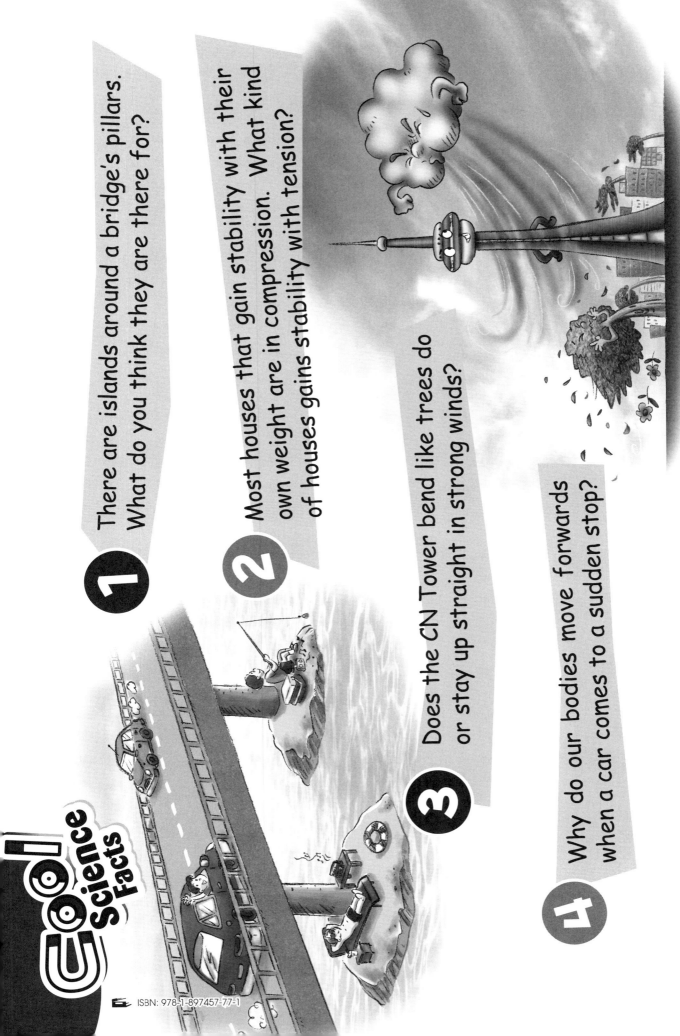

Cool Science Facts

1 There are islands around a bridge's pillars. What do you think they are there for?

2 Most houses that gain stability with their own weight are in compression. What kind of houses gains stability with tension?

3 Does the CN Tower bend like trees do or stay up straight in strong winds?

4 Why do our bodies move forwards when a car comes to a sudden stop?

Find the answers on the next page.

ISBN: 978-1-897457-77-1

Cool Science Facts

1

Although a bridge's pillars can withstand force from the load above them, they are vulnerable to impacts from things like ships. In 1946, part of the Cooper River Bridge in the U.S.A collapsed because a cargo ship ran into one of its pillars. To protect the bridge from future collisions, engineers built an island made of rocks around each pillar so that in case of a collision, the ship would hit the island first. The island slopes downwards into the river so that the ship will be stopped and gently pushed back into the river.

Cooper River Bridge

protection island

2

Tipis and other tents use tension as support. Instead of relying on the strength of the material (like brick or concrete) to keep it stable, the design of the tipi does the job. The tipi's frame of wooden poles, with fabric wrapped around it, makes a cone shape. This cone shape distributes the forces in a similar way as triangles do, making the tipi very stable even in strong winds.

ISBN: 978-1-897457-77-1

4

If your car is moving forwards at 50 km/h, your body is moving forwards at 50 km/h too.

Hitting the brake causes the car to stop as your body keeps moving. This happens because of inertia. Inertia is a tendency for things to keep moving until an external force stops them. Do you know what stops your body from moving forwards in a car?

Seatbelts apply the stopping forces.

3

The CN Tower, like all tall structures, bends with the wind. In high winds of 120 km/h, the antenna sways 1.07 m away from the vertical.

The CN Tower has a wind tolerance of 420 km/h. It is important that tall structures can bend a little bit. If they could not, very strong winds might push them over.

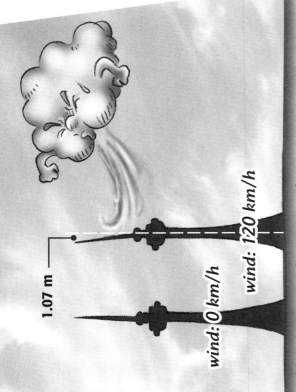

1.07 m

wind: 0 km/h

wind: 120 km/h

*Diagram is not drawn to scale.

ISBN: 978-1-897457-77-1

ISBN: 978-1-897457-77-1

Understanding
Matter and
Energy

ISBN: 978-1-897457-77-1

1 Matter and Energy

Take a look around you. What do you see? From ceilings to floors, from air to water, from trees to you, everything is matter. In this unit, you will explore matter and the common properties of matter.

It takes up space and it has weight. Please guess what it is!

After completing this unit, you will
- be able to identify matter.
- be able to describe the common properties of matter.
- know that some matter cannot be seen.

I know it is "matter", but many things in the world, even you and I, are matter. I need more clues before I can guess.

Vocabulary

matter: anything that takes up space and has mass

property: what an object looks like or how it behaves

Properties of a Metal Fork

texture: smooth
lustre: shiny
hardness: hard

ISBN: 978-1-897457-77-1

Can you identify the metal that is used to make pop cans? Yes, it is aluminum! Aluminum is the most abundant metal and its many useful properties make it widely used. It is a malleable metal, which means it can be rolled and pressed into paper-thin foil that you can use for baking. Moreover, unlike some other metals, aluminum does not rust. Aluminum is also an excellent material to use for the bodies of vehicles and aircrafts because it is lightweight. However, pure aluminum's high malleability also makes it insufficiently rigid for structures. Hence, small amounts of other metals, such as copper, are added to it to make it strong and durable.

Aluminum is a recyclable material, so make sure you put your pop cans into the recycling bin.

A. Fill in the blanks to complete the sentences. Then check the matter.

volume   weight
space

What is Matter?

- Matter has 1. __Weight__, which means it can be measured on a scale.

- Matter takes up 2. __space__, which means it has 3. __Volume__.

4.

- E light   F water power
- G rain   H conversation
- I friction   J ice

B. Match each term with its description. Then write the correct word to describe each item.

| lustre | solubility | clarity | malleability | viscosity | hardness | texture |

1 ~~solubility~~
the resistance of a substance to flow
(high/low)

honey: ✓

water: _____

2 ~~hardness~~
the capability of being shaped
(high/low)

clay: ✓

ice: _____

3 ~~lustre~~
the ability of a substance to dissolve
(high/low)

toothpaste: _____

sugar: ✓

4 ~~malleability~~
the ability to reflect light
(dull/shiny)

glass: ✓

carpet: _____

5 ~~hardness~~
the clearness of a substance
(transparent/translucent/opaque)

paper: _____

brick: ✓

6 ~~clarity~~
the way a surface looks and feels
(rough/spiky)

cactus: _____

tree bark: ✓

7 ~~hardness~~
the resistance of a solid to changing shape
(hard/soft)

rock: ✓

jelly: _____

ISBN: 978-1-897457-77-1

C. Complete what Jerry says.

As we know, matter is something that has
1. _Matter_ and takes up 2. _mass_ .
As air is invisible, it seems that air is not
matter. Let's study air to prove that air is
an example of 3. _Space_ .

matter
space
mass

D. Check the two pictures that prove air is matter. Then use the checked pictures to explain why air is matter.

An Insulated Mug

Weighing Balloons

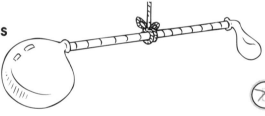

Weight of the Balloons

Balloons

30 g

Blowing Bubbles

Air Is Matter

1. **picture title**    _bacuause you blou_

2. **picture title** 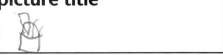   _bacuause it is hot_

2 States of Matter

Anything that takes up space and has mass is matter. Matter can exist in three states: solid, liquid, and gas. In this unit, you will investigate the three states of matter and the properties of each state.

After completing this unit, you will

- be able to identify and describe the three states of matter.

- know the properties of each state of matter.

Tom, I can't close this. Can you help me?

No, Jenny. Solids have definite volume. Even if you squeeze them, they take up the same amount of space.

Vocabulary

state: the physical form of matter

solid: has a definite volume and shape

liquid: has a definite volume and no definite shape

gas: has no definite volume or shape

gas
solid
liquid

ISBN: 978-1-897457-77-1

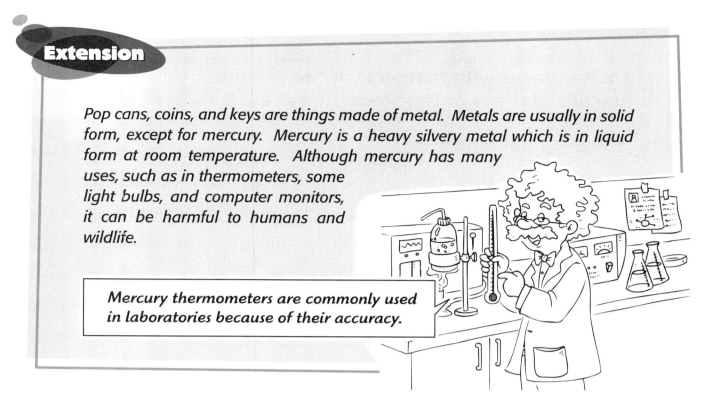

Pop cans, coins, and keys are things made of metal. Metals are usually in solid form, except for mercury. Mercury is a heavy silvery metal which is in liquid form at room temperature. Although mercury has many uses, such as in thermometers, some light bulbs, and computer monitors, it can be harmful to humans and wildlife.

Mercury thermometers are commonly used in laboratories because of their accuracy.

A. Name the three states of matter. Then draw lines to indicate the states of the items.

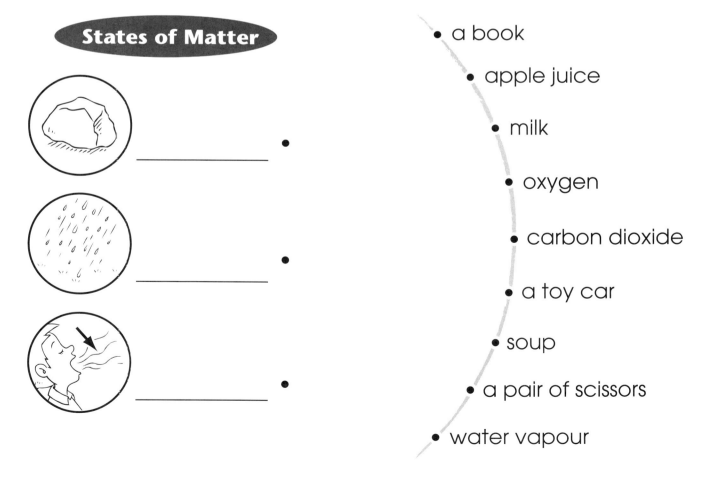

States of Matter

_____ •

_____ •

_____ •

• a book

• apple juice

• milk

• oxygen

• carbon dioxide

• a toy car

• soup

• a pair of scissors

• water vapour

B. **Fill in the blanks with "definite" or "no definite". Then draw lines to the descriptions of the properties of each state of matter.**

Solid

- _____ shape
- _____ volume

Liquid

- _____ shape
- _____ volume

Gas

- _____ shape
- _____ volume

- takes the shape of its container

- flows easily

- cannot flow

- fills its entire container regardless of its amount

- has a fixed volume and shape

C. **Identify the states of water. Then give an example to show how we use each state of water.**

When we take a shower, water is in its 1._____ state.

Example _____

When water is frozen into ice cubes, water is in its 2._____ state.

Example _____

The steam rising from a cup of tea is water in its 3._____ state.

Example _____

ISBN: 978-1-897457-77-1

D. Read the paragraph. Then answer the questions.

Most gases are colourless, but under special conditions, some gases produce light in amazing colours. Neon, helium, and argon are some of the gases that produce light when in close contact with electricity. Neon signs, as a matter of fact, are just that. A neon sign is plugged into an electrical socket, and the neon lights up, giving off orange or red light. Neon signs in other colours are actually made from other gases. Gold "neon" light, for example, is often helium, and purple "neon" light is often argon.

1. What is the state of matter of neon at room temperature? What makes it special?

   _____

   _____

2. What gases have similar features as neon?

   _____

   _____

3. In what conditions will some gases be lit up?

   _____

   _____

4. The neon sign is filled with different gases. Colour the parts with the correct colours.

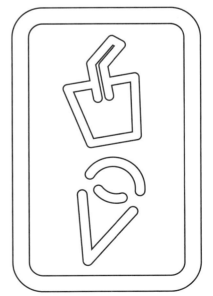

frame: neon
drink: argon
ice cream: helium

3 Changes in States of Matter

Solid, liquid, and gas are the three states of matter. Matter can go through changes of state when heat is added or taken away. In this unit, you will see how heat changes the states of matter.

After completing this unit, you will

- be able to describe how each state changes to another state.

- understand how heat changes the states of matter.

Mom, how long will it take the batter to become a solid, delicious cake?

Vocabulary

melting: change in state from solid to liquid

evaporation: change in state from liquid to gas

condensation: change in state from gas to liquid

freezing: change in state from liquid to solid

evaporating

melting

ISBN: 978-1-897457-77-1

On a hot summer day, it is nice to have a cold drink to cool you down. However, have you noticed that something is formed outside the container when your cold drink has been sitting out for a while?
It is water. The water droplets start to drip down the sides, making the container wet. Where do you think this water comes from?

(A) your hands   (B) the drink

(C) the air   (D) the glass

Answer: C

A. Describe the changes of state with the correct words. Then identify the change of state each picture shows.

Changes of State

1. [_____]
   liquid ➡ solid

2. [_____]
   gas ➡ liquid

3. [_____]
   solid ➡ liquid

4. [_____]
   solid ➡ gas

5. [_____]
   liquid ➡ gas

condensation   evaporation
melting   freezing   sublimation*

*sublimation: change in state from solid to gas

6. _____   7. _____

8. _____   9. _____

B. **Colour the arrows to show the heat added or taken away. Fill in the blanks with the given words. Then describe each situation.**

1.

Solid

melting

deposition*

evaporation

Liquid

Gas

condensation

sublimation

freezing

red: heat added

blue: heat taken away

*deposition: change in state from gas to solid

2.

heat _____ ;

added/taken away

_____

change of state

3.

heat _____ ;

_____

4. spraying water over an ice rink

heat _____ ; _____

5. mothball decreasing in size

heat _____ ; _____

6. steam escaping from a kettle

heat _____ ; _____

7. steam making a window foggy

heat _____ ; _____

ISBN: 978-1-897457-77-1

C. Read the paragraph. Then answer the questions.

When a solid is heated, it melts into a liquid. When more heat is added, the liquid evaporates into a gas. What will happen if a gas is heated vigorously? It will turn into the fourth state of matter – plasma. Plasmas are like gases, but plasmas are hotter and are even hot enough to emit light. Lightning is an example of plasma that occurs naturally. Stars in the night sky are another form of plasma. They are balls of plasma burning brightly from millions of kilometres away. Fluorescent light is an example of plasma too. When the light is turned on, the electricity flows through the gas inside the glass tube. The gas gets heated up to become plasma and gives off light.

Plasma!

1. Name the states of matter and give an example of each.

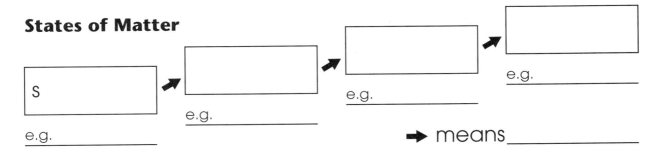

States of Matter

S

e.g.

e.g.

e.g.

e.g.

➡ means _____

2. How are plasmas related to gases?

_____

3. Give an example of plasma that does not occur naturally. Explain how it works.

_____

_____

Introduction

In the winter, water on roads changes its state from liquid to solid to form a layer of ice. This layer of ice makes it very dangerous to drive. To help keep roads from becoming icy, people spread salt on them. Do you know how salt helps keep roads from becoming icy?

Hypothesis

Sprinkling salt on ice causes it to melt

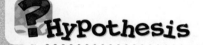

_____ .

faster/slower

Materials

- **2 ice cubes**
- **2 plates**
- **salt**

Steps

1. Put an ice cube on each plate.

2. Sprinkle salt on one of the cubes and leave the second one untouched.

ISBN 978-1-897457-77-1

3. Observe the ice cubes for two minutes.

4. Draw to record your observation.

┌─ **My observation** ──────┐
│   │
│   │
│   │
│   │
│   │
└───────────────────────────┘

without salt   **with salt**

Result

Which ice cube melted faster?

_____

┌─────────────────────────────┐
│ *Ice melts at 0˚C, but when salt* │
│ *is added to it, ice can melt at a* │
│ *temperature lower than 0˚C.* │
│ *This means that the ice starts to* │
│ *melt before it reaches 0˚C.* │
└─────────────────────────────┘

If lots of salt is added to an ice cube, do you think it will take less time for the ice to change into a liquid?

_____

Why do people put salt on roads?

_____

_____

Conclusion

The hypothesis was: _____

_____

My experiment _____ the
hypothesis.   supported/did not support

4 Measuring Matter

Everything is made of matter, but not all matter behaves in the same way. Some things are heavy, some are light, some are stretchable, and some are rough. In this unit, you will learn different ways to measure and describe matter.

After completing this unit, you will

- know the measurements that are used to describe matter.
- know what each measurement tells us about matter.
- understand the difference between mass and weight.

> Mrs. Karr, 45 kg is my weight on Earth. I would have a different weight if I were on the moon, but my height is still 1.2 m no matter where I am.

45 kg

1.2 m

Vocabulary

mass: measures the amount of matter in an object

weight: measures the effect that gravity has on mass

volume: measures the amount of space an object takes up

density: measures the amount of matter in a given space

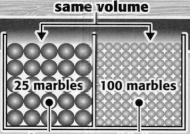

same volume

25 marbles | 100 marbles

lower density | higher density

ISBN: 978-1-897457-77-1

Extension

How would you weigh an elephant? Two thousand years ago in China, an elephant was sent to Cao Chong's home for his father, who was eager to find out its weight. Unfortunately, without measuring tools that could measure an animal that large, no one could think of a solution. However, Cao Chong had an idea. He asked his father to put the elephant on a boat and mark the water level. Then, the elephant was unloaded onto the shore and the boat was filled up with stones until the boat reached the marked line. Finally, the stones were weighed to find out the weight of the elephant. Everyone, including Cao Chong's father, was amazed with Cao Chong's intelligence, because Cao Chong was only six years old!

weight of
the elephant = weight of
the stones

A. Match each term with the correct description. Then write "the same" or "different" on the lines to compare the properties of the items.

| volume | mass |
| density | weight |

1. **Properties of an Object**

   • _____ : the amount of matter in an object

   • _____ : the effect that gravity has on mass

   • _____ : the amount of matter in a given space

   • _____ : the amount of space an object takes up

2.

   volume: _____

   weight: _____

   density: _____

3.

   volume: _____

   weight: _____

   density: _____

B. Read each scenario. Then describe the change of the different measurements with the given words.

> increased   decreased   stayed the same

1. A bowl filled with water was put into a freezer for 2 days. Ice formed and a bit of it stuck out from the bowl.

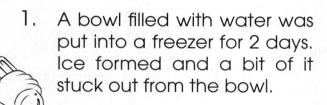

in a freezer
(2 days)

weight: _____

volume: _____

mass: _____

2. John deflated a blown up balloon. Then he filled the balloon with water until it reached the same size as before.

water

weight: _____

volume: _____

mass: _____

C. Unscramble the letters to fill in the blanks. Then indicate the relative density of each thing.

Any matter that has a higher density than water will 1._____ (iskn) , while matter with a lower density than water will 2._____ (tofla).

3.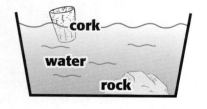

cork

water

rock

Density: _____
       lowest ➝ highest

4. Oil has a lower density than water.

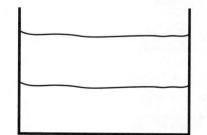

Colour:

oil – yellow

water – blue

D. Read the paragraphs. Then answer the questions.

Mass is a measurement in kilograms (kg) of the amount of matter an object contains. It is constant anywhere in the universe and can never be zero. Weight is a measurement in newtons (N) of an object's heaviness and is determined by the force of gravity acting on an object. It is not constant throughout the universe and it can be zero.

On Earth, an astronaut's mass is 60 kg and her weight is about 600 N (10 times her mass). On the moon, the force of gravity is one sixth of what it is on Earth. Therefore, if the astronaut steps onto the moon, her mass is still 60 kg, but her weight is now about 100 N.

1. **Mass** (unit: _____)

   - is a measure of _____

   - the mass of an object is _____ in the universe and can never be _____

2. **Weight** (unit: _____)

   - is a measure of _____

   - the weight of an object is _____ in the universe and can be _____

3. Calculate and record the mass and weight.

Earth

Moon

	Mass	Weight	
		on Earth	*on moon*
astronaut	60 kg	600 N	
pig		1200 N	
dog			20 N

5 Physical and Chemical Changes

A change in matter can be either a physical change or a chemical change. This change can be either reversible or irreversible. In this unit, you will identify different kinds of changes in matter and classify them as reversible or irreversible.

After completing this unit, you will

- be able to identify changes in matter as physical or chemical.

- be able to distinguish between reversible and irreversible changes in matter.

> *Sam, you shouldn't leave the table when you are using a toaster. The bread is burned and it is an irreversible change. You are wasting food!*

Vocabulary

physical change: change in the physical properties of matter

chemical change: change in the substance of matter

reversible: able to change back to original state

irreversible: unable to change back to original state

sliced: physical change

turning brown: chemical change

ISBN: 978-1-897457-77-1

Before a gumball becomes what you buy from stores, it goes through several changes of state. In the old days, the ingredient that made gum chewy was a resin found in trees, but the chewy substance is now made by humans instead. This human-made solid ingredient is heated, causing it to become a thin liquid, similar to syrup. Sugar and softeners are then added and mixed in by a large blender, giving the substance a doughy texture. Next, flavour is added and the gum goes through a long tube, allowing it to cool and become firmer. It is cut into sections and then formed into balls of different sizes. Finally, gumballs are coated with sugar and food colouring, turning them into the brightly coloured gumballs we love to chew!

The ingredient that makes the substance chewy is a trade secret, but I know there are waxes and fats in it.

A. Determine whether each description is about a "physical change" or a "chemical change". Then identify the examples of each type of change.

1.

a change of physical properties such as a change in size and shape

e.g. _____

2.

a change in which something new is formed; the new substance has different properties from the original materials

e.g. _____

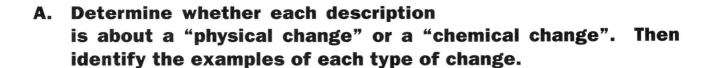

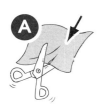 A  B  C  D  E  F

B.   Determine whether each change is "reversible" or "irreversible".

1.

_____

2.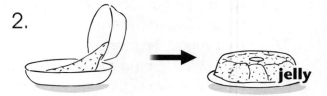

_____

3.

_____

4.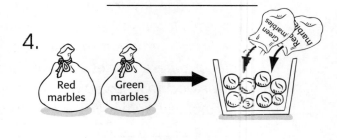

_____

C.   Determine whether each change is "reversible" or "irreversible" and whether it is a "physical change" or a "chemical change". Then give an example of your own.

1.

_____ ; _____ change

2.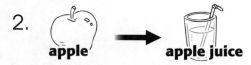

_____ ; _____

3.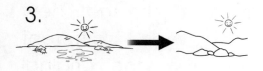

_____ ; _____

4.

_____ ; _____

5. Give an example of an irreversible physical change.

_____

ISBN 978-1-897457-77-1

D. Read the paragraph. Then answer the questions.

Baking a cake requires both chemical and physical changes. One chemical change happens in the baking powder. When baking powder is heated, it releases the gas carbon dioxide, which is what causes cake to rise. An important physical change is the one that is easy to see if you watch a cake

baking through an oven window: liquid batter becomes solid cake. Heat applied to dough while baking causes water in the liquid ingredients, like milk and eggs, to evaporate, leaving the solid ingredients behind.

1. Describe a chemical change and a physical change in baking cakes.

   Chemical change: _____

   Physical change: _____

2. There is one factor that affects both chemical and physical changes in baking cakes. What is it?

   _____

3. Determine the parts that undergo chemical and physical changes in a burning candle.

   Chemical change: _____

   _____

   Physical change: _____

   _____

6 Environmental Impacts

We make things from different materials for different purposes, depending on the properties of the materials. In this unit, you will investigate the environmental impacts associated with their production, use, and disposal.

After completing this unit, you will

- know how some products are made and the changes they undergo.

- understand how some common practices have negative impacts on our health and the environment.

Jenny, we should put our plastic bottles into the recycling bin so that they will have a smaller impact on the environment.

Vocabulary

iron ore: rocks that contain iron

slag: the residue formed by molten metal

iron nails

There are many things we can do to reduce our impact on the environment. Making things out of waste is a good way to reduce the amount of trash we send to landfills. You can make waste products useful again just by making physical changes. For example, you can make a bird feeder from an empty milk carton, or a candle holder from a glass jar. Before you throw something away, think of what physical changes you could make to create a new, useful product.

Cut out a window and put some bird seeds in the carton.

Clean the jar and put a candle inside.

A. Write "physical change" or "chemical change" in the arrows. Then fill in the blanks with "positive" or "negative".

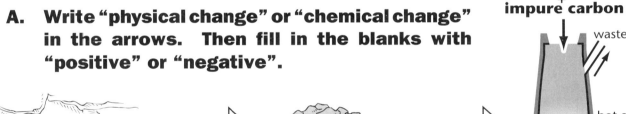

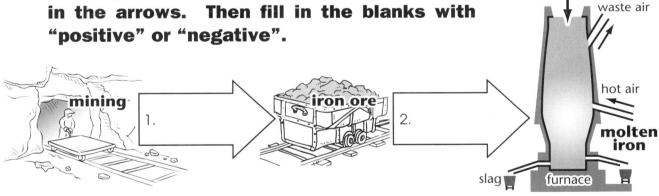

Explosives are used to break the rocks containing ores. This causes a 3._____ impact on the environment. Waste gases are produced during the extraction of iron. This causes a 4._____ environmental impact too. However, molten iron is moulded into different things or combined with carbon to become steel, which is an ideal material for construction. This has a 5._____ impact on our society.

ISBN: 978-1-897457-77-1

B. **Write "physical change" or "chemical change" in the boxes to complete the diagram. Then fill in the blanks.**

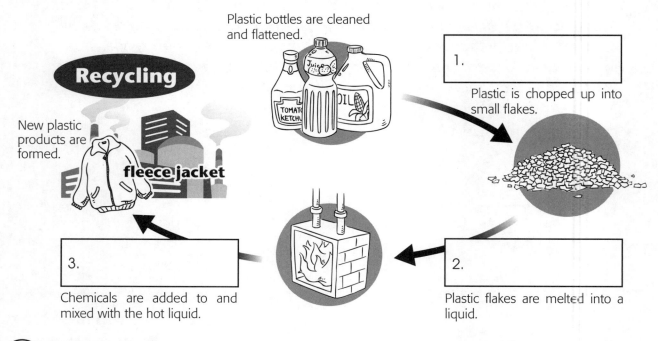

Plastic bottles are cleaned and flattened.

1. _____

Plastic is chopped up into small flakes.

New plastic products are formed.

Recycling

fleece jacket

3. _____

Chemicals are added to and mixed with the hot liquid.

2. _____

Plastic flakes are melted into a liquid.

:) **Positive Impacts on the Environment of Recycling Plastic Bottles:**

- Recycling can save 4._____ because it takes less energy to recycle
  <u>energy/time</u>
  used materials than to make them from scratch.

- It helps reduce the 5._____ on landfill sites and cuts down the
  <u>plants/pressure</u>
  amount of waste.

:(**Negative Impacts on the Environment of Recycling Plastic Bottles:**

- Recycling areas can become 6._____ because discarded plastics
  <u>clean/unhygienic</u>
  are often not well cleaned.

- Recycling plants may emit 7._____ substances and other pollutants
  <u>harmless/toxic</u>
  that cause air pollution.

- Plastic bottles can leach 8._____ substances that contaminate
  <u>harmful/useful</u>
  water, percolate into the ground, and 9._____ the groundwater.
  <u>pollute/freshen up</u>

ISBN: 973-1-897457-77-1

C. Read the paragraph. Then fill in the information.

Chemical preservatives in foods prevent or slow down the growth of microorganisms and mould, preserve the nutritional value and appearance of foods, and prolong the amount of time foods can be stored. The use of chemical preservatives gives us a lot of benefits, but the preservatives may have an impact on our health. Also, the packaging that preserved food requires affects the environment.

Functions: 1._____

_____

_____

_____

Chemical Preservatives Added

Dried Fruits

Special

Advantages of Adding Chemical Preservatives:

- 2._____ food is wasted, which
  Less/More
  reduces the amount of waste in landfills.

- Food is 3._____ to consumers anytime.
  limited/available

- 4._____ people get sick from eating spoiled food.
  More/Fewer

Disadvantages of Adding Chemical Preservatives:

- The preservatives may cause harm to our 5._____ .
  health/garden

- It creates a need for more 6._____ .
  food/packaging

- Lots of 7._____ is used to make chemical preservatives.
  light/energy

Experiment

Introduction

Baking cakes and burning candles are some chemical changes that improve our standards of living. Not all chemical changes are helpful though, and some are damaging. Did you know that rusting in metals is a chemical change? Rusting degrades metals and weakens structures. Is there anything that we can do to slow down this chemical change?

Hypothesis

Choose one substance. (substances: water, oil, vinegar, salty water)

An iron nail rusts slower in _____ than in other substances.

Steps

Materials

- a marker
- 4 yogurt cups
- 4 iron nails
- 4 liquids:
  water, oil, vinegar,
  salty water

1. Label each yogurt cup with the name of the liquid that it will be filled with.

2. Put an iron nail into each cup.

3. Fill each cup with its corresponding liquid so that each iron nail is completely covered. Then put all the cups under the sun.

ISBN: 978-1-897457-77-1

4. Observe the nails for 14 days and record the results.

5. You may need to refill the yogurt cups if they are drying out.

> Be patient. It might take longer than 14 days to see the changes.

| Day | ✔: rust   X: no rust | | | |
	water	oil	vinegar	salty water
1				
2				
3				
4				
5				
6				
7				
8				
9				
10				
11				
12				
13				
14				

Conclusion

The hypothesis was: _____

_____

My experiment _____ the
hypothesis.   supported/did not support

Try to complete this review in **30 minutes**.

30 minutes

This review consists of five sections, from A to E. The marks for each question are shown in parentheses. The circle at the bottom right corner is for the marks you get in each section. An overall record is on the last page of the review.

A. Write T for true and F for false.

1. Oil has lower viscosity than water. **(2)** _____

2. The greater the volume an object has, the greater its weight. **(2)** _____

3. 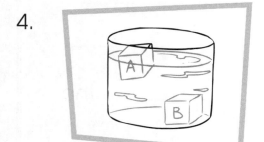 Mowing the grass is an example of an irreversible physical change. **(2)**

_____

4. Block A has a greater density than block B. **(2)**

_____

8

ISBN: 978-1-897457-77-1

B. Do the matching.

1.  (3) •

2. 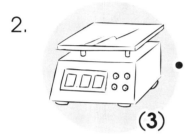 (3) •

3.  (3) •

4. 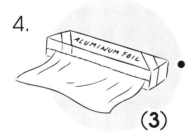 (3) •

5.  (3) •

• has high solubility

• shows evaporation

• measures weight

• shows a chemical change

• has high malleability

15

ISBN: 978-1-897457-77-1

C. Label the diagram and determine how heat is involved in each stage. Then describe the solid state of water (ice) and answer the questions.

1. **Three States of Water** (2 marks each)

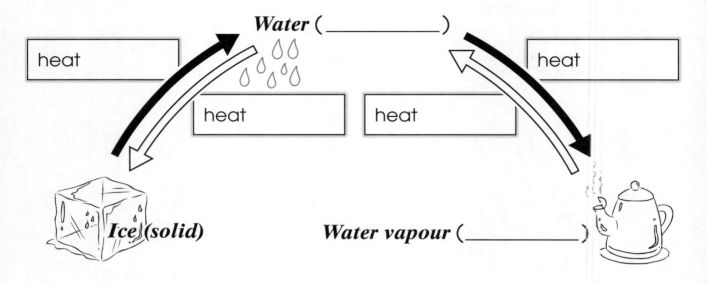

Water (_____)

heat

heat

heat

heat

Ice (solid)

Water vapour (_____)

2. Properties of Ice

- shape: **(2)**

   _____
   definite/not definite

- volume: **(2)**

   _____
   definite/not definite

- malleability: **(2)**

   _____
   high/low

- clarity: **(2)**

   _____
   translucent/opaque

- lustre: **(2)**

   _____
   dull/shiny

3. Identify what kind of change takes place when we crush ice.

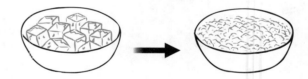

a. **physical / chemical** change **(2)**

   Reason: _____

   _____

   _____ **(3)**

b. **reversible / irreversible** change **(2)**

   Reason: _____

   _____

   _____ **(3)**

32

ISBN: 978-1-897457-77-1

D. **Read the experiments and look at the results in the diagrams. Then answer the questions.**

Sally has three jars of liquids:

Experiment 1

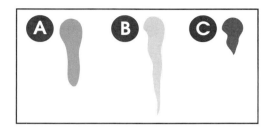

Sally puts a teaspoon of each kind of liquid on a piece of cardboard. Then she holds the cardboard vertically.

1. What property of matter is measured in this experiment?
    _____ **(2)**

2. What does this property measure? _____ **(2)**

3. Result of this experiment: _____
    _____ **(3)**

Experiment 2

 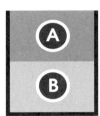

Sally puts two kinds of liquid, each with the same amount, into a container.

4. What property of matter is measured in this experiment?
    _____ **(2)**

5. What does this property mean? _____ **(2)**

6. Result of this experiment: _____
    _____ **(3)**

7.

The liquids I have are water, oil-based paint, and oil. Label the jars.

Jar A: _____ **(3)**

Jar B: _____ **(3)**

Jar C: _____ **(3)**

23

E. Answer the questions.

1. Write one positive impact and one negative impact that recycling aluminum cans has on the environment.

Positive impact: _____

_____ **(2)**

Negative impact: _____

_____ **(2)**

2. Describe the states and the change of the aluminum. Circle the correct answers.

a.

	(2)

heat added/taken away

molten aluminum

_____ **(2)**   _____ **(2)**

b. It is a **chemical / physical** change. **(2)**

c. The change is **irreversible / reversible** . **(2)**

3. Is aluminum an example of matter? Explain. **(4)**

_____

_____

4. Describe the properties of aluminum.

malleability: _____ **(2)**

clarity: _____ **(2)**

22

ISBN: 978-1-897457-77-1

My Record

Section A	8
Section B	15
Section C	32
Section D	23
Section E	22

Total 100

80-100

Great work! You really understand your science stuff! Research your favourite science topics at the library or on the Internet to find out more about the topics related to this section. Keep challenging yourself to learn more!

60-79

Good work! You understand some basic concepts, but try reading through the units again to see whether you can master the material! Go over the questions that you had trouble with to make sure you know the correct answers.

below 60

You can do much better! Try reading over the units again. Ask your parents or teachers any questions you might have. Once you feel confident that you know the material, try the review again. Science is exciting, so don't give up!

The Weather Specialist

In the old days when a drought persisted and crops withered, the only thing people could do was to pray for rain to fall. Now weather specialists have a better way to induce rain. It is called "cloud seeding". The process involves injecting silver iodide into a cloud. Cloud droplets will then stick to the particles of silver iodide and fall to the ground as rain.

Cloud seeding began in the 1940s. The earliest attempts at cloud seeding involved dropping pellets of crushed dry ice, or carbon dioxide, into the top of a cloud.

Cloud seeding is commonly used in China. Weather specialists there have induced rain in Beijing to help relieve drought and wash tons of dust from the Gobi desert that was dumped on the capital by sandstorms. Before the 2008 Olympic Games, Chinese weather specialists induced rain to clear the air of pollution in the city. Cloud seeding is also used to extinguish forest fires. Artificially induced rain has been used to help put out three big forest fires in north and northeast China.

ISBN: 978-1-897457-77-1

Cool Science Facts

Read the message

1 Do you know how "invisible ink" works?

2 What can we add to bread dough with yeast to stop it from rising?

3 Does wood melt under very high temperatures?

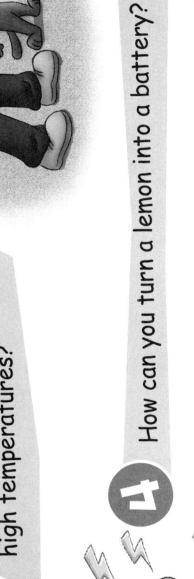

4 How can you turn a lemon into a battery?

5 How many times can you recycle a piece of paper?

Find the answers on the next page.

ISBN: 978-1-897457-77-1

Cool Science Facts

1

If you want to write a secret message on white paper, use an organic solution like milk and water. To read the message, expose the paper to heat by holding it under an incandescent light bulb or over a lit candle, and your message will turn brown. The colour change happens because the heat causes the milk to react with the oxygen in the air.

2

Salt does not stop bread from rising altogether but it makes bread rise less by making it harder for the yeast to do its work. Bread rises because yeast converts sugar into carbon dioxide bubbles. When bakers make bread, they put a little bit of salt into the dough so that it will not rise too much or have too many bubbles. The ideal dough should have about 2% salt, and if there is too much salt, it will kill some of the yeast and the bread will not rise.

ISBN 978-1-897457-77-1

4 Lemons and other acidic fruits can generate electricity when their acidic juice mixes with metals. Put a zinc screw and a copper screw inside a lemon and it will become a battery! If you attach a small LED light bulb to the screws with a wire, the bulb will light up.

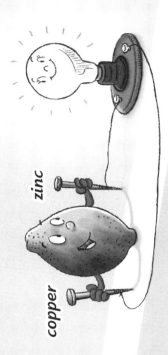

zinc

copper

3 No, wood does not melt at high temperatures. It is true that most solids melt (turn into liquids) when heated, but wood burns instead. The chemical change that takes place during burning turns wood into charcoal, another solid, instead of a liquid.

charcoal

5 You can recycle a piece of paper about 7 times before its wood fibres become too weak to hold together. Paper is made of many interlocking wood fibres. When you recycle paper, the paper is mixed with water and this mixture gets ground up in a blender. Every time paper goes through this process, its fibres get shorter, making it harder for them to hold together.

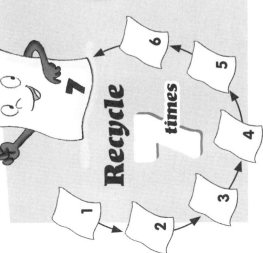

Recycle 7 times

ISBN: 978-1-897457-77-1

ISBN: 978-1-897457-77-1

Understanding
Earth and Space Systems

ISBN: 978-1-897457-77-1

1 Forms of Energy

Take a look around your home, school, and community; you will see that energy is everywhere. We use different forms of energy for different activities and purposes. In this unit, you will identify a variety of energy forms and give everyday examples for how different kinds of energy are used.

After completing this unit, you will

- know what energy is.
- be able to identify different forms of energy.
- know what potential energy and kinetic energy are.

Sammy, why have you been sitting there for so long?

kinetic energy

I don't want to lose my potential energy.

sound energy

energy: the ability to make things move and do work

potential energy: stored energy in an object

kinetic energy: the energy in things that are in motion

ISBN: 978-1-897457-77-1

Energy is everywhere. The sun gives off heat and light energy which make it possible for life to exist on Earth. Plants need light energy from the sun to make food, whereas we get our energy from the food that we eat. List 5 daily activities that require energy from the least energy needed to the most energy needed.

Activities by Energy Needed

least

_____

_____

_____

_____

greatest _____

It doesn't take much energy to walk.

A. Fill in the blanks. Then check the objects that need energy to work.

What is Energy?

Energy is the ability to 1._____
move/stay

and do work. For example, living

things need energy to 2._____;
waste/grow

a light bulb uses energy to

3._____ a room and an oven
illuminate/burn

uses energy to 4._____ food.
heat/cut

Objects that need energy to work:

A

B

C

D

E

B. Identify each form of energy and the object that uses that energy. Then give an example of each.

Form of Energy

1. [   ]

   - the energy that determines temperature

   - e.g. _____ and _____

2. [   ]

   - the energy that is used by electronics

   - e.g. _____ and _____

3. [   ]

   - the energy that is produced by vibrations

   - e.g. _____ and _____

4. [   ]

   - the energy that allows us to see things

   - e.g. _____ and _____

5. [   ]

   - the energy that keeps us from floating in the air

   - e.g. _____ and _____

6. [   ]

   - the energy that comes from the movement of an object

   - e.g. _____ and _____

electrical energy

heat energy

gravitational energy

light energy

mechanical energy

sound energy

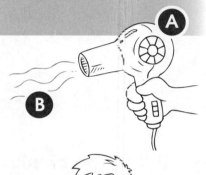

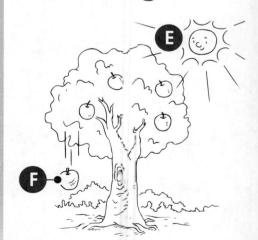

ISBN: 978-1-897457-77-1

C. Read the paragraph. Then complete the diagram.

Energy exists in many different forms, but all forms fall into two categories: potential energy and kinetic energy. Potential energy is the energy stored in an object, while kinetic energy is the energy in a moving object. Imagine a roller coaster with two peaks, the first higher than the second. At the top of the first peak, the cart has the most potential energy possible. As it descends, it releases its potential energy as kinetic energy until it reaches the lowest point, where it has the most kinetic energy possible. It then makes use of this kinetic energy to reach the second peak. The cart gains potential energy as it ascends but it still has some kinetic energy. On a roller coaster, energy changes from potential to kinetic energy and back again many times over the course of a ride.

1.

Energy

the energy stored in an object	the energy a moving object has

2.

P.E.: _____
K.E.: _____
high/low

_____ P.E.
_____ K.E.
gaining/losing

_____ P.E.
_____ K.E.
gaining/losing

P.E.: _____
K.E.: _____
high/low

2 Energy Sources

We now know that we use energy in different forms all the time but where does each energy form come from? For example, we know that a toaster uses electrical energy to produce heat energy, but where did it get its electrical energy? In this unit, you will look at various energy sources.

After completing this unit, you will

- be able to identify different energy sources.
- know where each source of energy comes from.
- know the characteristics of each kind of fossil fuel.

ORANGE JUICE

Good game so far! Here's an energy source to provide you with the energy you'll need for the rest of the game.

v o c a b u l a r y

energy source: wind

energy source:
a material that produces energy

ISBN: 978-1-897457-77-1

We know that plants get energy from the sun to grow and make their own food, but do you know how much energy the sun gives us? The sun gives off light, which allows us to see, and gives off heat to warm up the Earth. Can you feel the heat energy from the sun? On a hot, sunny day, hang a thermometer under the shade of a tree and hang another thermometer under the sun. After 1 hour, check and record the temperatures on the thermometers.

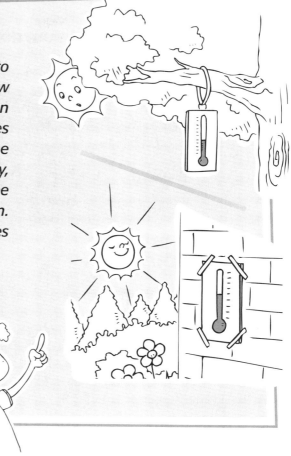

 under the shade of a tree: _____

under the sun: _____

Why aren't the temperatures shown on the two thermometers the same?

A. What make things work or grow? Write the letters in the circles.

1.

2.

3.

4.

5.

6.

A wind

B food

C the sun

D gasoline

E battery

F muscles

B. Name the energy source and complete the descriptions.

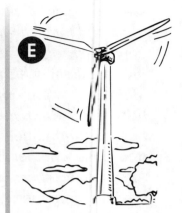

oil   biomass   coal   solar energy

wind energy   nuclear energy   hydroelectricity

mining   water   nuclear   rays

air   animal   mud

Energy Source

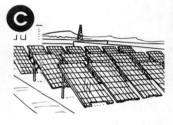

A _____ : formed under layers of _____ that covered remains of organic matter

B _____ : a fossil fuel extracted from the ground by _____

C _____ : comes from the sun's _____

D _____ : plant material and _____ waste that contain stored energy

E _____ : comes from moving _____

F _____ : comes from a natural flow of _____

G _____ : energy released by a _____ reaction

ISBN: 978-1-897457-77-1

C. Read the paragraph. Then answer the questions.

Combined, fossil fuels are the main source of the world's energy. All fossil fuels were formed in a similar way: the bodies of dead plants and animals were covered with layers of sediment millions of years ago. Millions of years of exposure to intense heat and pressure from inside the Earth fossilized their remains, changing them chemically. They became black goo (oil), gas (natural gas), or black, rock-like solids (coal). Since fossil fuels form beneath the Earth's surface, they can be difficult to reach: coal must be mined, and oil and natural gas must be drilled for. The different fossil fuels come from different types of plants and animals that were exposed to different amounts of heat and pressure during fossilization.

1. How are fossil fuels formed?

    _____

    _____

2. Read the descriptions. Name the fossil fuels and fill in the blanks.

Types of Fossil Fuels

a.	b.	c.
• _____ goo	• _____ solids	• gas
• can be obtained from drilling	• can be obtained from _____	• can be obtained from _____
• is commonly used for fuel	• is mainly used to generate _____ electricity/ideas	• is mainly used to _____ systems vacuum/heat

3 Renewable and Non-renewable Sources of Energy

All energy sources are either renewable or non-renewable. In this unit, you will learn about these two kinds of energy sources and identify some energy sources as renewable or non-renewable.

After completing this unit, you will

- know what renewable and non-renewable energy sources are.

- know the characteristics of some energy sources.

> *I have a calculator that stores energy during the day so that it can work at any time, even at night. What is its energy source?*

> *It is solar!*

EARTH

renewable energy source: geothermal energy

renewable energy source:
an energy source that will never run out

non-renewable energy source:
an energy source that is not replaced or is replaced only very slowly by natural processes

Ainsworth Hot Springs (British Columbia, Canada)

ISBN: 978-1-897457-77-1

Hydroelectric energy is produced by the force of moving water. Moving water is not the only way that we use water to make things work. People 200 years ago already knew how to use steam to make a locomotive move. Coal was the fuel used for heating the water in a locomotive. When heated, the liquid water turns to steam, which is gathered to push the piston that connects to the driving wheels to make the locomotive move. Water is an important energy source. Can you come up with an idea of using water power to do work at home?

A. Fill in the blanks with the given words.

examples

| replaced   natural   run | water   oil   sun |
| limited | natural gas |

Energy Sources

Renewable Energy Sources:

sources of energy that are generated by 1._____ resources that will never 2._____ out

e.g. 3._____

4._____

Non-renewable Energy Sources:

natural resources that cannot be 5._____ quickly and have a 6._____ supply

e.g. 7._____

8._____

B. **Sort the energy sources into the correct columns. Then draw lines to match the terms with the correct descriptions.**

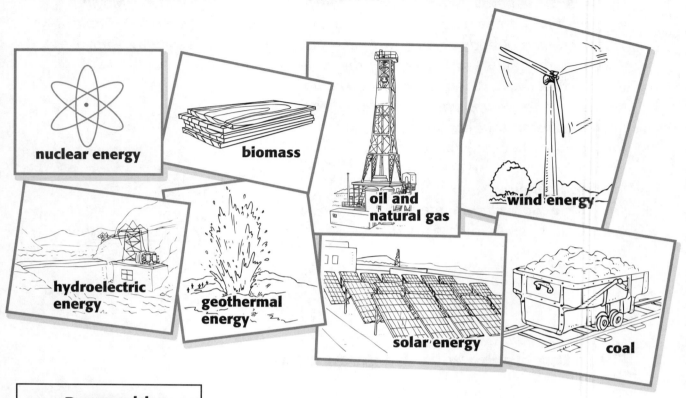

nuclear energy

biomass

oil and natural gas

wind energy

hydroelectric energy

geothermal energy

solar energy

coal

Renewable Energy Sources

_____

_____

_____

_____

_____

• reliable sources; provide steady energy supply

• unreliable sources; they rely heavily on geographical activities

• difficult to find the right site to capture natural resources

Non-renewable Energy Sources

_____

_____

_____

• will be depleted

ISBN: 978-1-897457-77-1

C. Read the paragraph. Then complete the diagram.

Biomass is a valuable renewable energy source that comes from non-fossil organic matter, such as wood, grass, and animal waste. In Canada, pulp and paper plants and saw mills are major users of biomass as an energy source. They use their own waste products, such as bark, wood chips, diseased or damaged trees, and sawdust, to generate electricity to meet both their own needs and the needs of the communities around them. Biomass can generate electricity in a number of ways, including burning it to heat water. This generates steam that causes turbines to turn and produce electricity. Mixing biomass with water and sealing it in a tank where it is digested by special bacteria produces a gas called biogas. This gas can then be used to generate electricity as well.

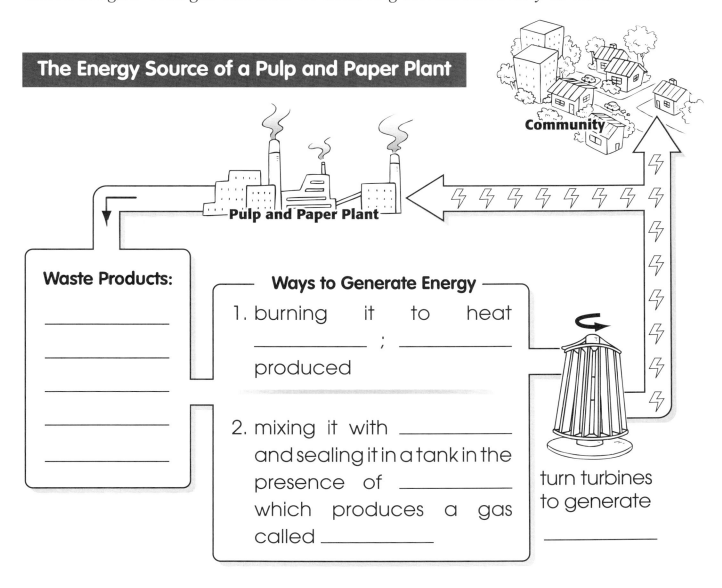

The Energy Source of a Pulp and Paper Plant

Community

Pulp and Paper Plant

Waste Products:

_____
_____
_____
_____

Ways to Generate Energy

1. burning it to heat _____ ; _____ produced

2. mixing it with _____ and sealing it in a tank in the presence of _____ which produces a gas called _____

turn turbines to generate _____

ISBN: 978-1-897457-77-1

Experiment

Introduction

Hydroelectric Power Plant in Niagara Falls

Hydroelectric power plants take advantage of the power of falling water to generate electricity. A dam is usually built across a river to store lots of water in the reservoir behind it. The water is carried through pipes to a waterwheel called a turbine that is connected to an electricity generator. How does a turbine take part in generating electricity?

Hypothesis

When water rushes into a turbine, it will cause the turbine to turn.

Materials

- an empty plastic 2-L bottle
- 3 strings
- a screwdriver
- scissors
- a pen

Steps

1.  Cut out the bottom part of the plastic bottle.

2.  Make six holes around the bottom of the cylinder with the screwdriver.

Get the help of a parent to do steps 1 and 2.

ISBN 978-1-897457-77-1

3. Use the pen to twist each hole so that all holes are slanted to one side.

4. Poke three holes along the top of the cylinder.

5. Thread a string through each hole. Then knot the strings together.

6. Hold the cylinder under running water. Observe the cylinder.

Result

Does the cylinder turn as the water flows out?

_____

_____

Conclusion

The hypothesis was: _____

_____

My experiment _____ the
hypothesis.   supported/did not support

ISBN: 978-1-897457-77-1

4 Storing and Transforming Energy

Energy cannot be created or destroyed, but can only be changed from one form to another or to even more than one form. In this unit, you will explore how energy is transformed into other energy forms, and how these new forms are used.

After completing this unit, you will

- understand how energy is transformed from one form to another.

- know that energy can be neither created nor destroyed.

muscular energy

chemical energy

It looks like you're about to run out of muscular energy. If you eat this sandwich, you'll have chemical energy that will transform into muscular energy.

energy transformation: the changing of energy from one form to another

windmill: transforms wind energy into mechanical energy

ISBN 978-1-897457-77-1

Have you ever gone camping with your family? Have you ever tried to cook food by burning twigs? If you have, you have experienced the transformation of energy. This transformation involves different kinds of energy.

How energy was transformed:

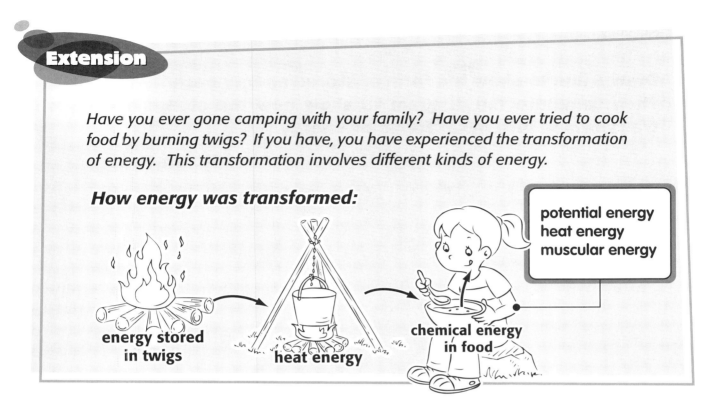

potential energy
heat energy
muscular energy

energy stored in twigs

heat energy

chemical energy in food

A. Determine the energy source each machine needs to function. Write the output energy.

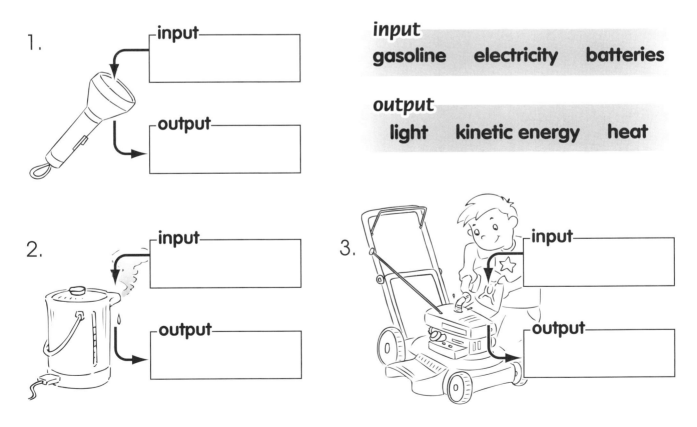

1.
input
output

input
gasoline   electricity   batteries

output
light   kinetic energy   heat

2.
input
output

3.
input
output

B. **Draw a line to show the form of stored energy each thing shows. Then complete the diagram to show how the stored energy is transformed into other forms of energy.**

1.

Stored Energy

rain falling down from the sky •

static electricity made
by brushing hair •

•

•

• gravitational energy

• chemical energy

• electrical energy

a lightning about to occur •

a ball sitting at the top of
the roof •

2.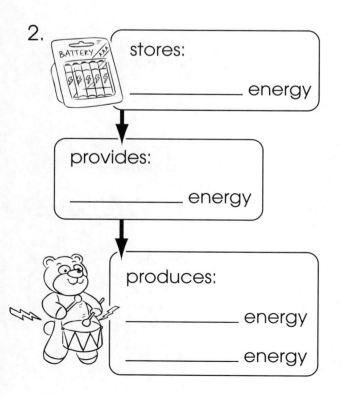

stores:

_____ energy

provides:

_____ energy

produces:

_____ energy

_____ energy

3.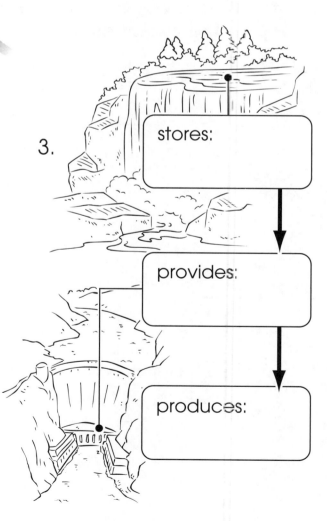

stores:

provides:

produces:

ISBN: 978-1-897457-77-1

C. Read the paragraph. Then answer the questions.

Energy may change from one form to another, but it can never be created or destroyed. The electricity that we use in our homes was not created by power plants, but it was transformed from the stored energy in fossil fuels or other resources. When we use electricity, we will not destroy it either. For example, when a fan is turned on, electrical energy is transformed into mechanical energy that turns the fan's blades. Through this mechanical energy, wind energy is produced. The turning of the blades also creates heat energy, but this is considered to be a wasteful by-product because we cannot use it.

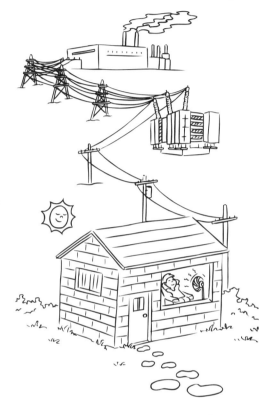

1. Complete the path to show how the energy is transformed.

fossil fuels
↓

-power plant-

-fan-

+

-by-product-

2. Describe how energy is transformed when you use a computer.

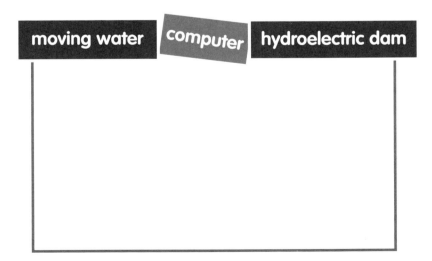

moving water | computer | hydroelectric dam

5 Impacts of Human Energy Use

The use of technology and consequently energy use have increased over the years. People nowadays rely heavily on the energy that is readily available to them. However, the use of energy has great impacts on our environment. In this unit, you will look at how our energy use impacts us and the Earth.

After completing this unit, you will

- know how energy improves our standards of living but also has negative impacts.

- know the environmental impacts of power plants.

> *Mom, there's a blackout tonight. How can I do my assignment?*

Vocabulary

power plant: place where electricity is generated from other forms of energy

power plant

ISEN: 978-1-897457-77-1

We have become accustomed to having electricity and hot water at our disposal whenever we need them. We turn on the lights when it gets dark, hop in the car when we need to get somewhere, and turn on the heat when we are cold. Think about a time before there was electricity and imagine how people lived then. Candles were their source of light in the dark. Horses were what they hopped onto to get to places, and fireplaces gave them warmth in winters. Can you come up with more differences between the lives of people in the past and people nowadays?

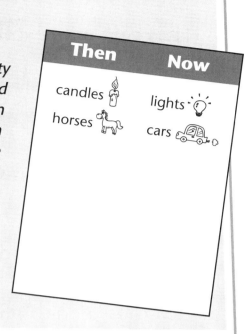

A. **Draw the happy or sad face in the circles to indicate whether the impacts of energy use are positive or negative.**

Positive 😊 and Negative 😦 Impacts of Energy

1. Energy provides us with a more convenient way of life than before. ◯

2. Being highly dependent on electricity leads to serious problems when a power outage occurs. ◯

3. Many power plants emit waste gases which are harmful to our health and the environment. ◯

4. Energy makes instant communication across the globe possible. ◯

5. Energy helps reduce the amount of time needed to travel. ◯

ISBN: 978-1-897457-77-1

B. Name each power station and its location. Circle the correct words.

Nuclear Hydroelectric	where water is channelled; resulting in fast water flow on a large amount of space and close to a lake or river

1. _____ Power Station

   Location: _____

   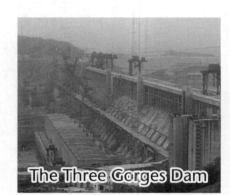
   The Three Gorges Dam

   Advantages
   - is a clean source of **non-renewable / renewable** energy
   - creates a new **threat / habitat** for wildlife
   - hydro dam helps control **floods / earthquakes** which could affect the people living downstream

   Disadvantages
   - **killed / fed** the existing vegetation during construction
   - results in power outage when water flow **increases / decreases**
   - **disrupts / encourages** salmon migration

2. _____ Power Station

   Location: _____

   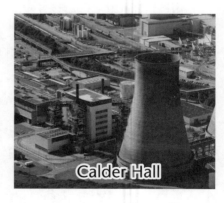
   Calder Hall

   Advantages
   - does not directly emit **carbon dioxide / oxygen** that pollutes air
   - has **low / high** energy yield of nuclear fuels

   Disadvantages
   - releases waste heat that causes the temperature of a nearby body of water to **increase / decrease**, harming aquatic life
   - the radioactive waste remains **active / inactive** for centuries, which may cause health risks

ISBN: 978-1-897457-77-1

C. Read the paragraphs. Then write three advantages and three disadvantages of fossil fuels.

There are many disadvantages and advantages of using fossil fuels. Of the disadvantages, many involve the environment: carbon dioxide from fossil fuel emissions may be contributing to climate change; extracting fossil fuels from the earth destroys habitats and displaces people; fossil fuels are also non-renewable, which means that they are going to run out.

The main advantage of fossil fuels is that they release a lot of energy when they are burned. Another advantage is that fossil fuels are inexpensive to produce and use compared to other energy sources. Finally, the supply of fossil fuel energy is more stable than energy from other sources like wind, the sun, and moving water.

The Mohare Power Station in Nevada

Advantages of Fossil Fuels

* _____

* _____

* _____

Disadvantages of Fossil Fuels

* _____

* _____

* _____

6 Energy Conservation

Most of our energy resources are non-renewable, which means they cannot be replaced easily. Although renewable energy can be replaced, it is expensive to produce and use. Hence, we should use our energy wisely. In this unit, you will learn why you should conserve energy and some ways to do it.

After completing this unit, you will
- know why we should conserve energy.
- know some ways to conserve energy.

> Mom, we should get this washer/ dryer combo. It uses about 30% less energy than the regular washers and dryers.

Vocabulary

energy conservation: reducing energy consumption by decreasing energy use or using it efficiently

double pane window
keeps air cool in summer and warm in winter

ISBN: 978-1-897457-77-1

Have you ever heard the expression "spring forward, fall back"? This refers to the practice of Daylight Saving Time. We set our clocks one hour ahead near the start of spring and then back one hour when fall begins. By doing so, we gain an hour of daylight during spring and summer. Since the sun can give us natural light for longer into the evenings, we use less artificial light and save energy. Many countries around the world follow Daylight Saving Time for this reason.

one hour ahead

What activities do you do during the longer hours of sunlight in the spring and summer?

A. Fill in the blanks to find the reasons for conserving energy. Then give one reason of your own.

Reasons for Conserving Energy:

replaced   greenhouse gases   consumption
pollute   non-renewable   global warming

1. Fossil fuels are _____ and will be used up within decades if we do not hold back on our _____ .

2. To generate electricity, large amounts of _____ are emitted from power plants.

3. Waste gases from vehicles _____ the environment and contribute to _____ .

4. Renewable energy can be _____ , but is often expensive and difficult to store.

5. **My Input** _____

   _____

B. **Circle the correct words and give your own suggestion on how to conserve energy. Then identify each person's problem and suggest a solution to him or her.**

1. **Ways to Conserve Energy**

 Use **energy-saving / traditional** light bulbs.

 Take a short **shower / rest** instead of a bath.

 Walk or travel by **car / bike** whenever you can.

 Turn **on / off** the lights when you are not using them.

 Turn the thermostat **up / down** during winter when you are going to bed or are not at home.

 Put on clothing to keep warm instead of turning **up / down** the heat.

 Use **natural / artificial** light instead of **natural / artificial** light whenever possible.

my idea _____

2. Problem: _____

_____

Suggestion: _____

_____

Mrs. Winter

3. Problem: _____

_____

Suggestion: _____

_____

Mr. Winter

The house is not warm enough because air leaks through gaps around the windows and doors.

Mrs. Winter   Mr. Winter

My colleague and I live close to each other, but it is more convenient for us if we drive our own cars to work.

C. **Read the paragraph. Write the features of Agbar Tower described in the paragraph. Then write three environmentally friendly features of the Gherkin.**

Architects adopt environmentally friendly designs to build buildings. There are many energy efficient buildings around the world. The Agbar Tower in Barcelona, Spain was built with certain features that help minimize energy use. This office tower has 4500 windows that allow natural light and ventilation into the building. Instead of relying on air conditioning to cool the building, temperature sensors were installed to regulate the opening and closing of window blinds. The windows are also double glazed to prevent heat from escaping. People often compare the Agbar Tower to the Gherkin in London, England. Do you know what makes the Gherkin energy efficient?

Agbar Tower

Location: _____

Environmentally Friendly Features:

_____

_____

_____

_____

Environmentally Friendly Features:
(Look for information in books or on websites.)

_____

_____

_____

The Gherkin

ISBN: 978-1-897457-77-1

 **Experiment**

Introduction

Sound is all around us. The sound from a TV or the music that we play is a form of sound energy. Since energy cannot be created, which form of energy transforms into sound energy? When I hit a drum, I hear sound. How does kinetic energy transform into sound energy?

Hypothesis

Kinetic energy   can / cannot   transform into sound energy by causing air vibrations.

Steps

1. Remove the lid of the jar and stretch the food wrap tightly over its opening.

Materials

- *an empty jar*
- *a piece of food wrap*
- *an elastic band*
- *black pepper*
- *a metal pot*
- *a metal spoon*

2.
food wrap

elastic band

Secure the food wrap with the elastic band. Make sure it is stretched tightly.

   ISBN: 978-1-897457-77-1

3. Sprinkle some black pepper over the food wrap.

4. Hit the bottom of the metal pot with the spoon.

| Hold the metal pot close to the jar to see the results. |

5. Observe what happens to the pepper.

Result

What happens to the pepper when the pot is hit?

_____

How do you know that the air is vibrating?

_____

_____

Conclusion

The hypothesis was: _____

_____

My experiment _____ the
hypothesis.   supported/did not support

Try to complete this review in **30 minutes**.

30 minutes

This review consists of five sections, from A to E. The marks for each question are shown in parentheses. The circle at the bottom right corner is for the marks you get in each section. An overall record is on the last page of the review.

A. Write T for true and F for false.

1. Wind, water, and oil are all renewable sources of energy. **(2)** _____

2. An energy source is either renewable or non-renewable. **(2)** _____

3.

The energy that turns a windmill is electrical energy. **(2)**

_____

4.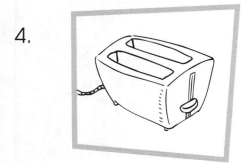

The light energy produced in a toaster is a wasteful by-product. **(2)**

_____

8

ISBN: 978-1-897457-77-1

B. Do the matching.

1.
(3)

2.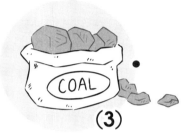
(3)

3.
(3)

4.
(3)

5.
(3)

- a kind of fossil fuel

- needs gasoline to work

- produces a source of biomass

- power supply depends on water flow

- an energy-efficient product

15

ISBN: 978-1-897457-77-1

C. Name and determine whether each energy source is renewable or non-renewable. Describe the source. Then answer the questions.

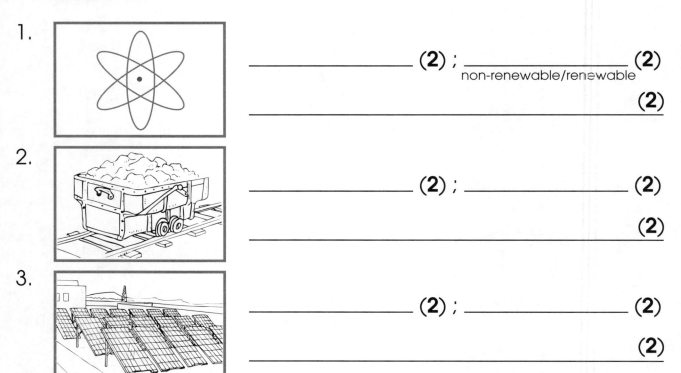

1. _____ **(2)** ; _____ **(2)**
   non-renewable/renewable

   _____ **(2)**

2. _____ **(2)** ; _____ **(2)**

   _____ **(2)**

3. _____ **(2)** ; _____ **(2)**

   _____ **(2)**

4. Write an advantage and a disadvantage of using each kind of energy source.

   Renewable
   ☺ _____ **(2)**
   ☹ _____ **(2)**

   Non-renewable
   ☺ _____ **(2)**
   ☹ _____ **(2)**

5. Mrs. Smith wants to produce energy herself for home use. Which of the above energy sources can she consider? Explain. **(3)**

   _____

   _____

29

ISBN 978-1-897457-77-1

D. **Identify the forms of energy involved when a roaster oven is at work. Describe their relationships. Then answer the questions.**

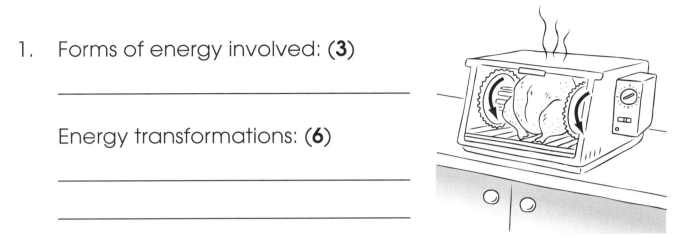

1. Forms of energy involved: **(3)**

    _____

    Energy transformations: **(6)**

    _____

    _____

2. The power plant not only provides energy for the oven to make it work, it also helps prevent floods. Identify this kind of power plant and describe it.

    Power plant: **hydroelectric / solar / nuclear** **(2)**

    Location: _____ **(2)**

    Another advantage of using it: _____ **(2)**

3. Write a positive impact and a negative impact of energy use on the environment.

    🙂 _____ **(2)**

    🙁 _____ **(2)**

4. Write the transformations of energy from a roast chicken you eat to your action of letting go of an elastic band. **(8)**

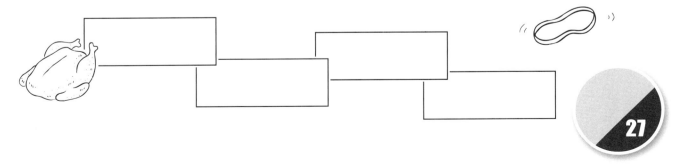

27

ISBN: 978-1-897457-77-1

E. **The boy is wasting energy. Write four things that he should do to conserve energy. Then answer the questions.**

1. **Things to Do to Conserve Energy**

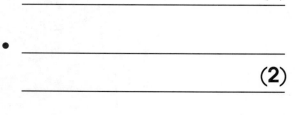

- _____ (2)

- _____ (2)

- _____ (2)

- _____ (2)

2. Give two reasons for conserving energy. **(4)**

_____

_____

3. Name three forms of energy you find in the picture and describe each form.

- _____ (2)

- _____ (2)

- _____ (2)

4. Describe the energy transformations involved when a traditional light bulb is turned on. Then identify one of its wasteful by-products. **(3)**

 _____

_____

21

ISBN 978-1-897457-77-1

My Record

Section A	8
Section B	15
Section C	29
Section D	27
Section E	21

Total

100

80-100

Great work! You really understand your science stuff! Research your favourite science topics at the library or on the Internet to find out more about the topics related to this section. Keep challenging yourself to learn more!

60-79

Good work! You understand some basic concepts, but try reading through the units again to see whether you can master the material! Go over the questions that you had trouble with to make sure you know the correct answers.

below 60

You can do much better! Try reading over the units again. Ask your parents or teachers any questions you might have. Once you feel confident that you know the material, try the review again. Science is exciting, so don't give up!

ISBN: 978-1-897457-77-1

The Astronaut

Curious about what it is like to work and live in space? You would have the chance to travel to space and experience working and living in space if you become an astronaut.

Bob Thirsk

Astronauts are specially trained to explore space. They can be scientists, teachers, doctors, or pilots. Before they can fly in space, astronauts have to undergo hundreds of hours of training. They learn about space technology and science, and basic medical skills. They also learn about the special tasks they have to perform in their missions. They have to be familiar with the state of weightlessness, too.

Roberta Bondar, a medical doctor by profession, is the first Canadian woman astronaut. In 1992, she flew on a space mission aboard the Discovery space shuttle and performed experiments in life and material sciences in space. Bob Thirsk, another Canadian astronaut, lived and worked on the International Space Station for six months with five other astronauts. He was the crew's medical officer and robotics specialist. In his mission, he performed scientific experiments and maintained and repaired the station.

ISBN 978-1-897457-77-1

Cool Science Facts

1 Can a vehicle run on the vegetable oil you use for cooking instead of gasoline?

2 How do energy-saving light bulbs save energy?

3 What can you do to reduce your house's energy consumption?

A. Never turn on heat or air conditioning.
B. Plant trees near your house.
C. Go outside often and fan your house.

4 Windmills should be put in the windiest spots. Where are these spots?

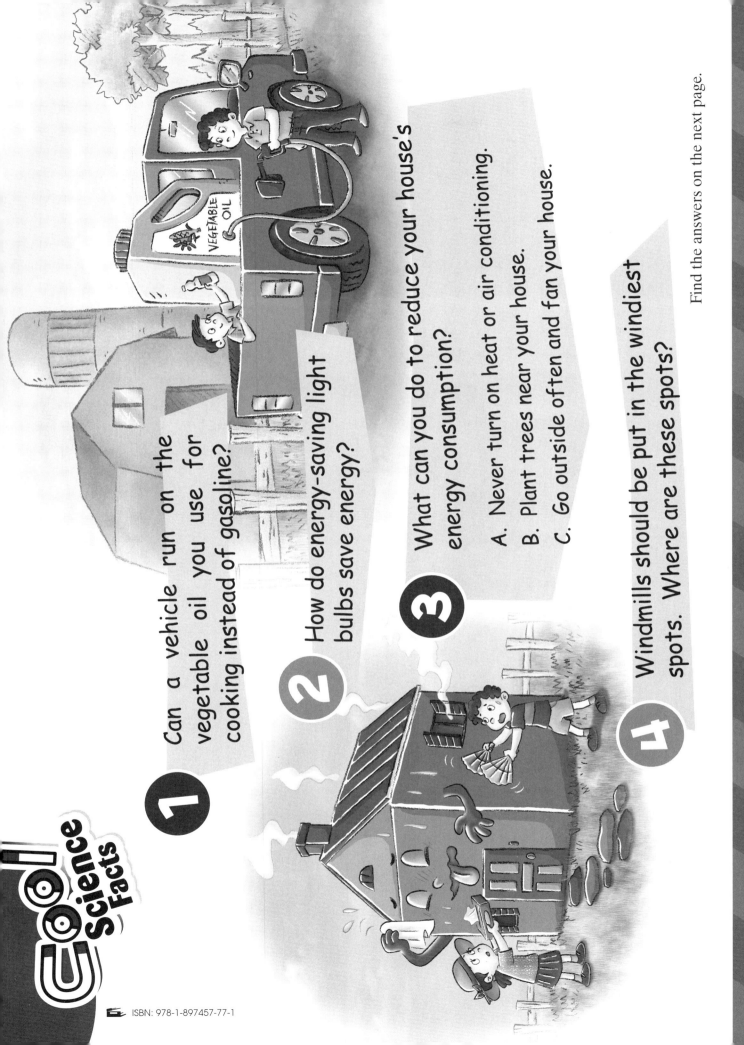

Find the answers on the next page.

ISBN: 978-1-897457-77-1

Cool Science Facts

1

Yes, you can run vehicles with diesel engines (not the ones with gasoline engines) on vegetable oil. Since vegetable oil is a lot thicker than conventional diesel fuel, it has to be pre-heated in a modified oil tank to reduce its viscosity. Then the heated vegetable oil can be used to power the vehicle.

Vegetable oil does not emit harmful chemicals into the air. You can also use biodiesel, which is a fuel manufactured from vegetable oil and alcohol.

2

Incandescent (traditional) light bulbs work by creating heat. The light they produce is just a by-product of this heat. Fluorescent (energy-saving) light bulbs produce light directly because of a chemical reaction inside them. This chemical reaction does not produce much waste heat, making fluorescent bulbs very efficient.

POPULAR SUPERMARKET

$5.99

$1.99

ENERGY SAVING

ISBN 978-1-897457-77-1

Answer: B

3

If you live in the northern hemisphere, consider planting a deciduous tree on the west side of your house. During the summer months, the shadow of the tree that is cast on the house will cool down the house and reduce the need for air conditioning. In the winter, the tree will lose its leaves and allow the sun to shine through and warm up the house. It also helps block some of the cold winds and reduce the need for heating.

Thank you, Mr. Tree.

4

The wind over oceans and lakes is very strong because there are no high mountains and tall buildings that slow it down. This is why windmills are often located on the coast. However, scientists in Europe and Britain are going one step further by placing windmills in the ocean. The windmills float on the water surface and, to keep them in place, they are anchored to the ocean floor. The energy produced gets transmitted back to land via underwater cables.

ISBN: 978-1-897457-77-1

ISBN: 978-1-897457-77-1

Answers

ISBN: 978-1-897457-77-1

Answers

1 Digestive System

A. 1. organs   2. breaks
   3. function   4. food
   5. nutrients   6. waste

B. 1. mouth
     mouth ; saliva ; swallow
   2. esophagus
     esophagus
   3. stomach
     stomach
   4. small intestine
     Nutrients
   5. colon
     water ; large
   6. rectum
     waste ; rectum

C. 1. A cow has just one stomach, but it is made up of four compartments.
   2. Ruminants are mammals that can digest indigestible food because they regurgitate and chew their food over and over.
   3. rumen ; bacteria
     reticulum ; mouth ; chamber
     omasum ; water ; minerals
     abomasum ; juices ; nutrients

2 Skeletal System

A. Check: A, C, F, G

B. 1. blood vessel
   2. marrow
   3. hollow
   4. blood cells

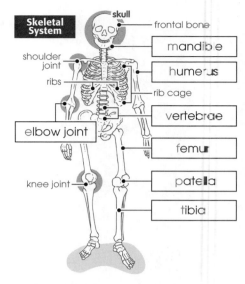

Skeletal System — skull, frontal bone, mandible, humerus, rib cage, vertebrae, femur, patella, tibia, shoulder joint, ribs, elbow joint, knee joint

   5. femur

C. 1. skull   2. rib cage
   3. (Any two of the following three)
     knee joint, shoulder joint, elbow joint

D. 1a. spinal cord   b. vertebrae
   2. The spine is a column of bones that runs down your back.
   3. The spine helps hold up the body and protects the spinal cord.

E. 1a. make new bone tissue so that bones can grow and repair themselves
     b. break down old bone tissue
     c. osteoclasts   d. osteoblasts
     e. osteoblasts   f. osteoclasts
   2a. blood   b. bone
     c. extra-thick ; thickness

3 Respiratory System

A. 1. two   2. rib cage
   3. lobes   4. three
   5. left   6. bigger

B. 1. nasal cavity   2. cleaned
   3. larynx   4. tube
   5. trachea   6. lungs

ISBN: 978-1-897457-77-1

7. bronchiole
8. bronchial tubes
9. diaphragm
10. muscle

C. (Colour the arrows accordingly.)
1. nose and mouth
2. nasal cavity
3. larynx
4. bronchial tubes
5. bronchioles
6. lungs
7. bronchioles
8. bronchial tubes
9. larynx
10. nasal cavity
11. nose and mouth
12. in the lungs

D.1a. oxygen   b. gills
    c. Oxygen   d. operculum
    e. carbon dioxide
    f. carbon dioxide

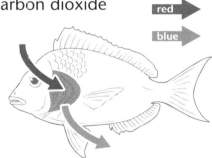

2a. lungs   b. skin

Experiment
(Individual experiment outcome)

4 Circulatory System

A. heart ; fist
arteries ; away
veins ; back
blood ; nutrients

B. 1. four   2. atrium
    3. ventricle   4. left
    5. Valves

C. 1. lungs   2. lungs
    3. body   4. rich
    5. atrium   6. valve
    7. valve   8. aorta
    9. Veins   10. atrium
   11. right   12. lungs
   13. carbon dioxide
   14. oxygen

D. 1. heart-lung
    2. carbon dioxide ; oxygen
    3. sick ; donor
    4. South Africa
    5. the United States
    6. Canada
    7. died
    8. the United States
    9. child
   10. alive

5 Nervous System

A. 1. brain   2. spinal cord
    3. nerves
    soft ; skull ; wrinkled ; 1.5 kg ; control

B. 1. cerebrum   2. biggest
    3. voluntary   4. messages
    5. memories   6. cerebellum
    7. coordination   8. brain stem
    9. spinal cord   10. involuntary
   11. spinal cord   12. nerves

C.

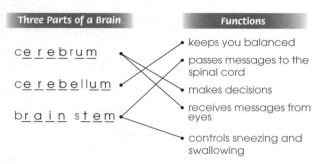

Three Parts of a Brain	Functions
cerebrum	keeps you balanced
cerebellum	passes messages to the spinal cord
brain stem	makes decisions
	receives messages from eyes
	controls sneezing and swallowing

D. 1. involuntary activities
   2. (Individual example)
   3.

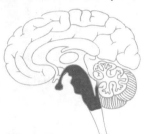

   brain stem
   4. voluntary activities
   5. (Individual example)
   6.

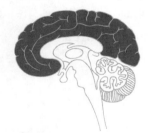

   cerebrum

E. 1a. brain   b. spinal cord
   c. spinal cord   d. muscles

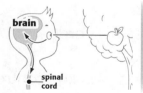 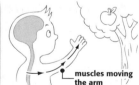

   2a. spinal cord   b. muscles

c. something that your body does without you thinking about doing it

6   Human Health and Diseases

A. 1. environmental
   Check: B, C, D
   2. social
   Check: A, B, C

B. 1. muscles   2. airways
   3. large   4. hole
   5. epilepsy   6. nervous
   7. asthma   8. respiratory
   9. atrial septal defect
   10. circulatory
   11. appendicitis
   12. digestive

C. sleep
   healthy
   protective
   hydrate ; waste
   radiation ; skin
   muscles ; increase
   (Individual example)

D. 1.

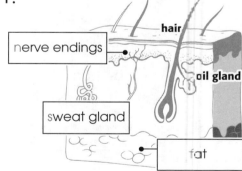

(Suggested functions)
epidermis ; produces melanin
dermis ; works closely with the nervous system
hypodermis ; keeps you warm

2a. melanin   b. UV rays
c. UV rays   d. melanin
3. The extra melanin produced during sun exposure causes your skin to get darker.

Experiment
(Individual experiment outcome)

Review
A. 1. T   2. F
3. F   4. F
B. 1.
(3)
2.
(3)
3.
(3)
4.
(3)
5.
(3)

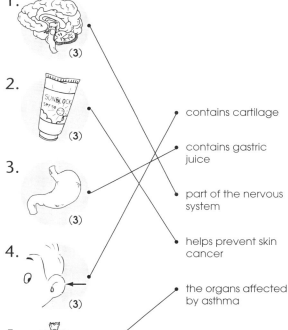

- contains cartilage
- contains gastric juice
- part of the nervous system
- helps prevent skin cancer
- the organs affected by asthma

C. 1. skeletal
(Any one of the following three)
skull, rib cage, spine
It provides body structure, protects organs, makes new blood cells,

and allows for body movement.
2. nervous ; brain
It receives information from the body and sends out instructions.
3. respiratory ; lungs
It obtains oxygen from the inhaled air and removes the carbon dioxide in the blood by exhaling.
4. circulatory ; heart
It passes nutrients and oxygen to different parts of the body and removes wastes.
D.1a. esophagus   b. small intestine
c. rectum   d. mouth
e. esophagus   f. stomach
g. small intestine
h. large intestine
i. rectum
2. It processes food and breaks it down into nutrients that our body needs. It also prepares waste to be removed.
3. It breaks down the food we eat with the enzymes in its gastric juice.
4a. voluntary ; cerebrum
b. involuntary ; brain stem
E. 1a. trachea   b. lungs
c. esophagus   d. stomach
2.

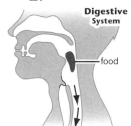

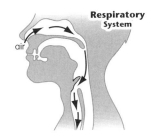

3. The movement is involuntary. It is controlled by the nervous sytem.

Answers

Section 2

1 Effects of Natural Forces

A.

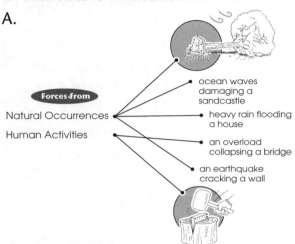

Forces from
Natural Occurrences
Human Activities

- ocean waves damaging a sandcastle
- heavy rain flooding a house
- an overload collapsing a bridge
- an earthquake cracking a wall

B. 1. tornado ; wind
2. earthquake ; surface
3. snowstorm ; snow
4. tsunami ; waves
5. flood ; rain
6. hurricane ; wind

C.1a. flexible   b. Brick
    c. crisscrossing   d. steel
   2a. drainage   b. masts
    c. curved   d. higher
    e. masts
   3a. shutters   b. in
    c. roof   d. slope
    e. water

D.1a. truss   b. beam
    c. rafter   d. joist
    e. joist   f. beam
    g. stud   h. foundation
2. It prevents damage to the structure caused by the accumulation of rain and snow on the roof.
3. Check: C
The triangular supports can provide more support than the vertical ones.

2 Impacts on Structures

A. 1. concrete ; skyscraper
2. grass ; tent
3. sand ; sandcastle
4. gravel ; playground
5. ice ; igloo

B. 1. heat ; expands ; lift up from
2. foundation ; uneven ; Cracks ; water
3. pillars ; rocks ; Insulate
4. The hotel's structure will be weakened and it will collapse.
5. No, it is not a good idea because skyscrapers must be built on a sturdy foundation, such as concrete ground.
  6a. The ice under the road melted and refroze causing the road to crack.
    b. Check: A

C. 1.

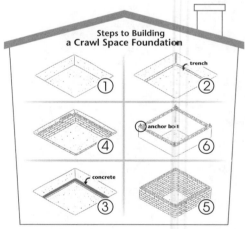

Steps to Building
a Crawl Space Foundation

① ② trench
④ ⑥ anchor bolt
③ concrete ⑤

2. A crawl space keeps the house's wooden frame off the ground. It also provides easy access to heating, plumbing, and electrical systems.
3. Concrete is used for building foundations because when it dries, it becomes hard and sturdy. It also does not rust.

    ISBN 978-1-897457-77-1

3 External and Internal Forces

A. 1a. external   b. internal
   2a. external   b. internal
   c. external   d. internal

B. 1a. live load   b. dead load
   2. dead ; weight of materials used in a structure
     live ; object that carries a load
   3. live ; natural force
     live ; object that carries a load
     dead ; weight of materials used in a structure
     dead ; structural item

C. 1.

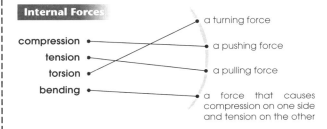

   2a. tension   b. compression
   c. bending   d. tension
   e. compression   f. torsion
   3. compression
   4. torsion
   5. tension
   6. bending

D. 1. Wood is used because wood is a sturdy material and it is lightweight.
   2. books ; wood pieces
3&4a. compression   b. tension
   c. bending   d. compression
   e. tension   f. bending
   5. Heavier books should be placed on the lower shelf. This will lower the bookshelf's centre of gravity, making it more stable.

Experiment

(Individual experiment outcome)

4 Bridges and Forces

A. 1. truss bridge ; D
   2. arch bridge ; B
   3. beam bridge ; C
   4. suspension bridge ; A

B. 1. beam

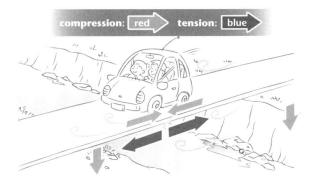

   a. live load   b. dead load
   c. live load
   2. arch

   a. live load   b. live load
   c. dead load
   3. Check: A, C, D, E

C. 1a. truss   b. truss

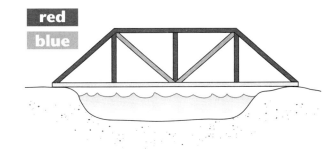

Answers

2a. suspension   b. tower
   c. cable   d. suspender

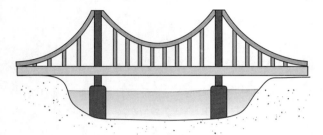

   3. bending ; compression ; tension

D. 1. 1: Push a caisson straight down into the water until it reaches the bottom while the top stays above the water's surface.

     2: Riverbed sediment inside the caisson gets dug out until the bedrock is reached.

     3: Concrete in liquid form is poured into the caisson, which now acts as a mould of the pillar.

     4: Within weeks, the concrete hardens and is strong enough to support a bridge.

   2. Check: A, B, D, E, F

5   Mechanical Systems

A. (Suggested examples)
   1. inclined plane ; ramp
   2. lever ; nutcracker
   3. wheel and axle ; bicycle wheel
   4. pulley ; pulley on a flagpole
   5. screw ; bottle cap
   6. wedge ; door stopper

B. 1. Lever: $60 \div 20 = 3$
           3 ; 10
     Inclined Plane: $80 \div 20 = 4$
                   4 ; 10

   2. 6 ; 8 N

3. 4 ; 50 N
4. 3 ; 20 N
5. less

C. 1.

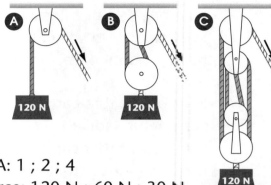

   MA: 1 ; 2 ; 4
   Force: 120 N ; 60 N ; 30 N
   2. C   3. less
   4. Check: C

D. 1. (Suggested examples)
   a. second

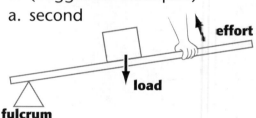

     nutcracker ; bottle opener ; wheelbarrow
   b. first

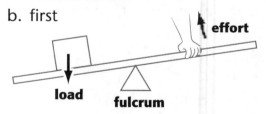

     scissors ; trolley ; see-saw
   c. third

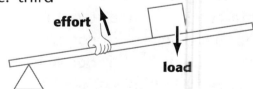

     tweezers ; pair of tongs ; broom
   2. A: wheel and axle ; first-class
      B: wedge ; third-class

ISBN 978-1-897457-77-1

6 Protective Equipment

A. (Suggested answers)
1. knee pads ; rib pad ; shoulder pads ; helmet
2. snowsuit ; helmet
3. elbow guards ; knee pads ; helmet ; wrist guards

B. 1. the respiratory system by preventing dust and sand from entering the lungs
2. the eyes from flying dust and sand
3. the ears from the loud noise made by the drilling machine
4. the hands by preventing cuts that might occur when handling construction materials
5. the feet from falling objects with the steel plate, and prevent punctures with the sole plate
6. the head and the brain from falling objects
7. A miner's helmet has a lamp mounted on the front of it. This lamp provides the lighting that a mine lacks.

C. 1. leather boots ; rubber boots
Leather boots provide the protection and comfort a miner needs, whereas a sewage worker needs a pair of boots that are waterproof with non-slippery soles.
2. clear goggles ; light protection goggles
Clear goggles allow the chemist to see clearly and prevent chemicals from striking the eyes. Light protection goggles protect one's eyes from the brightness of the welding area.

3. disposable gloves ; heavy cotton gloves
Disposable gloves help prevent the spread of germs and viruses. Heavy cotton gloves provide flexibility of movement and protect the hand from getting cut.
4. safety helmet ; streamlined helmet
A safety helmet protects the head from falling objects while a streamlined helmet protects the head and reduces air resistance.

D. 1. A: helmet ; plastic, foam
head and ears
B: face mask ; metal or plastic
facial features
C: shoulder pads ; plastic, foam
shoulders, upper back, collar bones, and ribs
D: gloves ; leather, nylon
hands and wrists
E: hockey pants ; nylon, foam
spine, kidneys, tailbone, and thighs
F: shin pads ; plastic, foam
lower legs
G: skates ; plastic, leather, nylon
feet
2. The plastic distributes the force from the external impact while the foam absorbs the shock.
3. No, we cannot. A hockey player needs thick padding in the helmet for increased warmth and protection, which a bicycle helmet does not provide.

Experiment

(Individual experiment outcome)

Answers

Review

A. 1. F   2. T
   3. F   4. F

B. 1.

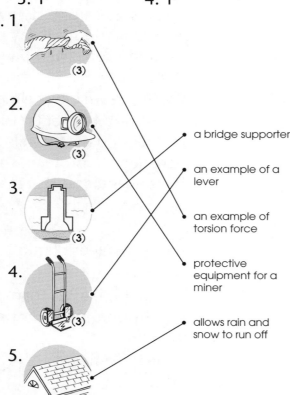

- a bridge supporter
- an example of a lever
- an example of torsion force
- protective equipment for a miner
- allows rain and snow to run off

C. 1. F ; C
     B ; D
     E ; A

2. Arch bridges are suited to be made only with concrete.

3. (Suggested answers)
     wind
     beam

D.1a. live load   b. live load
    c. live load   d. dead load
2. concrete
3. compression
4. live load
5. inclined plane
6. MA = 180 ÷ 30 = 6
    Force needed = 60 ÷ 6 = 10
    6 ; 10 N

E. 1. pulley
   2. one
   3. 50 N
   4. There will be two supporting ropes and two pulleys.
  5a. leather gloves ; protect hands from getting cuts
    b. steel-toe boots ; protect feet from falling objects and prevent punctures
    c. helmet ; protects head from falling objects

Section 3

1 Matter and Energy

A. 1. weight   2. space
   3. volume   4. Check: C, D, G, J

B. 1. viscosity ; high ; low
   2. malleability ; high ; low
   3. solubility ; low ; high
   4. lustre ; shiny ; dull
   5. clarity ; translucent ; opaque
   6. texture ; spiky ; rough
   7. hardness ; hard ; soft

C. 1. mass   2. space
   3. matter

D. Check: B, D
   1. Weighing Balloons ; Both balloons weigh the same, but the inflated one is heavier because of the air inside it. This shows that air has mass.
   2. Blowing Bubbles ; The bubbles are made by blowing air into them. This shows that air takes up space.

ISBN 978-1-897457-77-1

2 States of Matter

A.

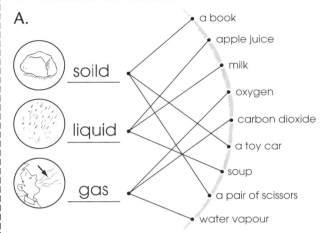

soild — a book, apple juice, milk, oxygen, carbon dioxide, a toy car, soup, a pair of scissors, water vapour

liquid

gas

B.

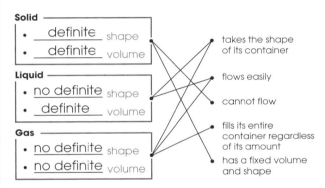

Solid
- __definite__ shape
- __definite__ volume

Liquid
- __no definite__ shape
- __definite__ volume

Gas
- __no definite__ shape
- __no definite__ volume

takes the shape of its container

flows easily

cannot flow

fills its entire container regardless of its amount

has a fixed volume and shape

C. (Individual examples)
1. liquid 2. solid 3. gas

D. 1. Neon is in its gas state at room temperature. It gives off orange or red light when it is in contact with electricity.
2. Helium and argon have similar features as neon.
3. Some gases will be lit up when they are in close contact with electricity.
4.

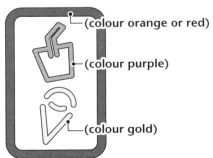

(colour orange or red)

(colour purple)

(colour gold)

3 Changes in States of Matter

A. 1. freezing 2. condensation
3. melting 4. sublimation
5. evaporation 6. condensation
7. melting 8. evaporation
9. freezing

B. 1.

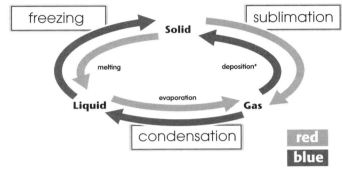

freezing | sublimation
Solid
melting | deposition*
Liquid | evaporation | Gas
condensation

red
blue

2. added ; melting
3. added ; evaporation
4. taken away ; freezing
5. added ; sublimation
6. added ; evaporation
7. taken away ; condensation

C. 1. (Individual examples)

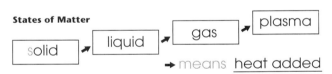

States of Matter

solid → liquid → gas → plasma

→ means heat added

2. Plasmas are gases that have been heated up.
3. When a fluorescent light is turned on, the electricity flows through the gas inside the glass tube. The gas gets heated up to become plasma and gives off light.

Experiment

(Individual experiment outcome)

ISBN: 978-1-897457-77-1

Answers

4 Measuring Matter

A. 1. mass ; weight ; density ; volume
 2. the same ; different ; different
 3. the same ; different ; different

B. 1. stayed the same ; increased ; stayed the same
 2. increased ; stayed the same ; increased

C. 1. sink   2. float
 3. cork, water, rock
 4.

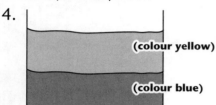

(colour yellow)

(colour blue)

D. 1. kilogram ; the amount of matter an object contains ; constant ; zero
 2. newton ; an object's heaviness that is determined by the force of gravity ; not constant ; zero
 3.

	Mass	Weight	
		on Earth	on moon
astronaut	60 kg	600 N	100 N
pig	120 kg	1200 N	200 N
dog	12 kg	120 N	20 N

5 Physical and Chemical Changes

A. 1. physical change ; A, D, E
 2. chemical change ; B, C, F

B. 1. irreversible   2. reversible
 3. irreversible   4. reversible

C. 1. irreversible ; chemical
 2. irreversible ; physical change
 3. reversible ; physical change
 4. irreversible ; chemical change
 5. (Individual example)

D. 1. Chemical change: Baking powder releases carbon dioxide when heated.
 Physical change: Water in the batter evaporates, leaving the solid ingredients behind.
 2. Heat affects both kinds of changes.
 3. Chemical change: The wick undergoes a chemical change when burning.
 Physical change: The wax undergoes a physical change from solid to liquid.

6 Environmental Impacts

A. 1. physical change
 2. chemical change
 3. negative
 4. negative
 5. positive

B. 1. physical change
 2. physical change
 3. chemical change
 4. energy   5. pressure
 6. unhygienic   7. toxic
 8. harmful   9. pollute

C. 1. prevent or slow down the growth of microorganisms and mould, preserve nutritional value and appearance, and prolong the amount of time foods can be stored
 2. Less   3. available
 4. Fewer   5. health
 6. packaging   7. energy

Experiment

(Individual experiment outcome)

ISBN: 978-1-897457-77-1

Review

A. 1. F   2. F
   3. T   4. F

B. 1.

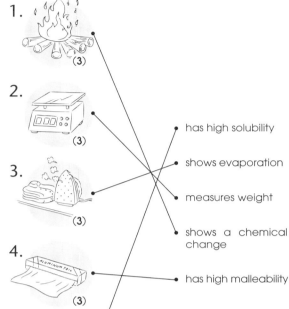

2.

3.

4.

5.

- has high solubility
- shows evaporation
- measures weight
- shows a chemical change
- has high malleability

C. 1.

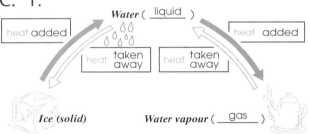

Water (liquid)

heat added

heat taken away   heat taken away

heat added

Ice (solid)   Water vapour (gas)

2. definite ; definite ; low ; translucent ; shiny

3a. physical ; There is only a change in shape and size, but no change in substance.

   b. reversible ; The crushed ice can be melted and then frozen into ice cubes again.

D. 1. Viscosity is measured.

   2. the resistance of a substance to flow

3. Liquid B has the lowest viscosity and liquid C has the highest viscosity.

4. Density is measured.

5. the amount of matter in a given space

6. Liquid A has the lowest density and liquid C has the highest density.

7. oil ; water ; oil-based paint

E. 1. (Suggested answers)
Positive:
Recycling aluminum cans reduces the pressure on landfill sites.
Negative:
Discarded aluminum cans are often not well cleaned, so recycling areas can become unhygienic.

2a.

heat added

heat added/taken away   molten aluminum

solid   liquid

   b. physical   c. reversible

3. Yes, aluminum is an example of matter because aluminum takes up space, and has weight and volume.

4. high ; opaque

Section 4

1   Forms of Energy

A. 1. move   2. grow
   3. illuminate   4. heat
   Check: B, C, E

B. (Individual examples)
1. heat energy ; B or E
2. electrical energy ; A
3. sound energy ; D
4. light energy ; E

5. gravitational energy ; F
6. mechanical energy ; C

C. 1.

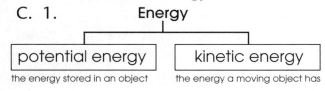

Energy

potential energy	kinetic energy
the energy stored in an object	the energy a moving object has

2.

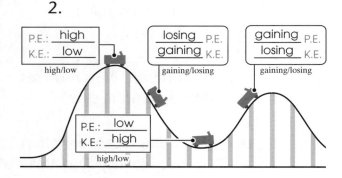

P.E.: high
K.E.: low
high/low

losing P.E.
gaining K.E.
gaining/losing

gaining P.E.
losing K.E.
gaining/losing

P.E.: low
K.E.: high
high/low

2 Energy Sources

A. 1. A 2. D 3. F
   4. E 5. C 6. B

B. A: oil ; mud
   B: coal ; mining
   C: solar energy ; rays
   D: biomass ; animal
   E: wind energy ; air
   F: hydroelectricity ; water
   G: nuclear energy ; nuclear

C. 1. They are formed by the bodies of dead plants and animals that were covered with layers of sediment. These remains are exposed to intense heat and pressure from inside the Earth for millions of years.

   2a. oil ; black
   b. coal ; black ; mining ; electricity
   c. natural gas ; drilling ; heat

3 Renewable and Non-renewable Sources of Energy

A. 1. natural 2. run
   3. water 4. sun
   5. replaced 6. limited
   7. oil 8. natural gas

B.

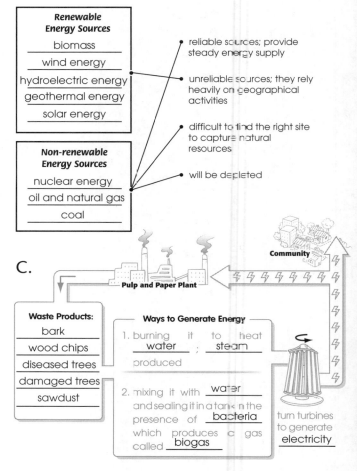

Renewable Energy Sources
biomass
wind energy
hydroelectric energy
geothermal energy
solar energy

Non-renewable Energy Sources
nuclear energy
oil and natural gas
coal

• reliable sources; provide steady energy supply
• unreliable sources; they rely heavily on geographical activities
• difficult to find the right site to capture natural resources
• will be depleted

C.

Community

Pulp and Paper Plant

Waste Products:
bark
wood chips
diseased trees
damaged trees
sawdust

Ways to Generate Energy
1. burning it to heat water ; steam produced
2. mixing it with water and sealing it in a tank in the presence of bacteria which produces a gas called biogas

turn turbines to generate electricity

Experiment
(Individual experiment outcome)

4 Storing and Transforming Energy

A. 1. batteries ; light
   2. electricity ; heat
   3. gasoline ; kinetic energy

ISBN 978-1-897457-77-1

B. 1.

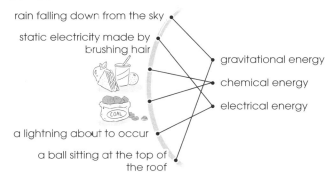

rain falling down from the sky

static electricity made by brushing hair

a lightning about to occur

a ball sitting at the top of the roof

gravitational energy

chemical energy

electrical energy

2. chemical ; electrical ; mechanical ; sound
3. gravitational energy ; mechanical energy ; electrical energy

C. 1. electrical energy ; mechanical energy ; wind energy ; heat energy
2. The gravitational energy in moving water becomes mechanical energy to turn turbines in a hydroelectric dam. The hydroelectric dam produces electricity to run a computer, which produces light, sound, and heat energy.

5 Impacts of Human Energy Use

A. 1. ☺ 2. ☹ 3. ☹
4. ☺ 5. ☺

B. 1. Hydroelectric ; where water is channelled; resulting in fast water flow ; renewable ; habitat ; floods ; killed ; decreases ; disrupts
2. Nuclear ; on a large amount of space and close to a lake or river ; carbon dioxide ; high ; increase ; active

C. Advantages:
release lots of energy when burned ; inexpensive to produce and use compared to other energy sources ; supply more stable than some other energy sources
Disadvantages:
carbon dioxide from emissions may contribute to climate change ; extracting fossil fuels destroys habitats and displaces people ; they are going to run out (non-renewable)

6 Energy Conservation

A. 1. non-renewable ; consumption
2. greenhouse gases
3. pollute ; global warming
4. replaced
5. (Individual answer)

B. 1. energy-saving ; shower ; bike ; off ; down ; up ; natural ; artificial (Individual answer)
2. Problem: Warm air escapes, hence more energy is needed for heating. Suggestion: Seal the gaps to keep warm air in.
3. Problem: More cars on the road means more gasoline is consumed. Suggestion: Reduce gasoline consumption by carpooling.

C. Barcelona, Spain
It has 4500 windows that let in natural light and ventilation. Temperature sensors regulate the opening and closing of window blinds. Windows are double glazed to prevent heat from escaping. (Individual findings)

Experiment

(Individual experiment outcome)

Review

A. 1. F   2. T
   3. F   4. T

B. 1.

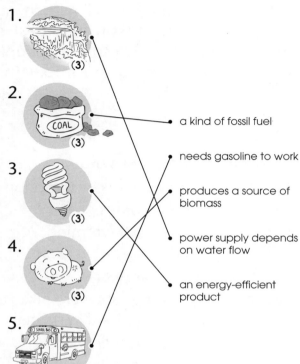

C. 1. nuclear energy ; non-renewable ; energy released by a nuclear reaction
   2. coal ; non-renewable ; a fossil fuel extracted from the ground by mining
   3. solar energy ; renewable ; comes from the sun
   4. Renewable:
      Advantage: will never run out
      Disadvantage: unreliable sources; rely heavily on geographical activities
      Non-renewable:
      Advantage: reliable sources; provide steady energy supply
      Disadvantage: will run out

5. She can consider solar energy because it is readily available. Also, solar panels take up a small space and can be easily installed.

D. (Suggested answers)
   1. electrical, heat, and light energy ; Electrical energy is transformed into heat energy, which then gets transformed into light energy.
   2. hydroelectric ; where there is consistent fast water flow ; it creates a new habitat for wildlife
   3. Positive: Energy provides us with a more convenient way of life.
      Negative: Many power plants emit harmful waste gases.
   4. chemical energy ; potential energy ; muscular energy ; kinetic energy

E. 1. Put on warm clothing instead of turning up the heat. ; Use natural light instead of artificial light. ; Close the refrigerator door. ; Turn off the toaster because it is not in use.
   2. Fossil fuels will get used up someday if we do not hold back on our consumption. Also, to generate electricity, large amounts of greenhouse gases are emitted.
   3. electrical energy: is used by electronics and electrical appliances
      light energy: allows us to see things
      sound energy: is produced by vibrations
   4. Electrical energy is transformed into heat energy, which is then transformed into light energy. The heat energy is a wasteful by-product.

ISBN: 978-1-897457-77-1

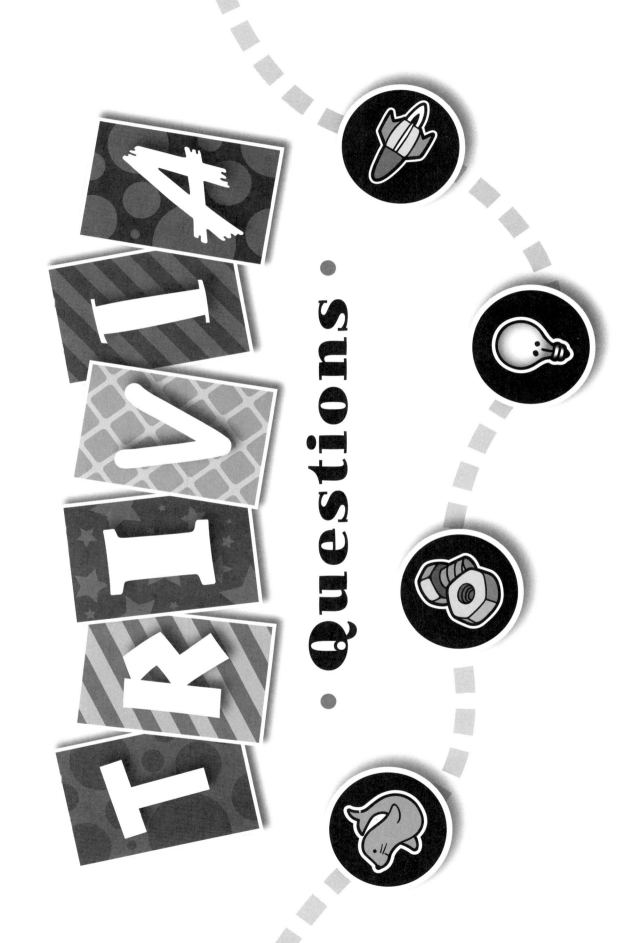

TRIVIA

• Questions •

ISBN: 978-1-897457-77-1

ISBN: 978-1-897457-77-1

About how long does it take for sunlight to reach the Earth?

A. 8 seconds

B. 8 minutes

C. 8 days

True or False

A camel's hump stores water.

True or False

All animals have brains.

True or False

We see smoke when we breathe outdoors in cold weather because our bodies produce smoke to keep us warm.

Answer:

B. 8 minutes

Answer:

false

A camel's hump stores fat. If a camel's fat were all over its body like human's fat is, the camel would get too hot and would sweat out its water.

Answer:

false

For example, jellyfish do not have brains. They have nerves in their skin, but no central nervous system.

Answer:

false

The air we exhale is warmer than the cold outside air. The cold air cools the exhaled air rapidly and mist, which looks like smoke, is formed.

ISBN: 978-1-897457-77-1

Where would you find the hardest substance in your body?

A. fingernails
B. teeth
C. bones

True or False

The longest man-made structure is the Great Wall of China.

True or False

The sun is hotter than a bolt of lightning.

The Statue of Liberty turned green due to a chemical change. What was its original colour?

A. yellow
B. copper
C. silver

Answer:

B. teeth

The enamel that covers your teeth is the hardest substance in your body.

Answer:

true

The Great Wall stretches over 6400 km across mountains and deserts.

Answer:

false

A bolt of lightning is five times hotter than the surface of the sun.

Answer:

B. copper

The statue's copper coating turned green due to the chemical reaction of the copper with the oxygen in the air.

ISBN 978-1-897457-77-1

Which planet is closest in size to our moon?

A. Jupiter
B. Mercury
C. Saturn

About how long do our red blood cells live?

A. two years
B. one day
C. three weeks
D. four months

True or False

Natural gas smells like rotten eggs because that is where it comes from.

True or False

Lunar soil is similar to the soil on Earth.

Answer:

B. Mercury

Answer:

false

Natural gas is odourless. A chemical is added to it to make it smell like rotten eggs so that we can easily detect leaks to prevent fires or explosions.

Answer:

D. four months

But don't worry, because your bones are constantly making new red blood cells to replace them.

Answer:

false

Unlike soil on Earth, lunar soil does not contain any air, water, or organic matter.

ISBN: 978-1-897457-77-1

What is the red spot on Jupiter?

A. a giant storm

B. a volcano

C. a giant ruby

D. a fire

True or False

A traditional fluorescent light bulb uses most of its electrical energy to produce light.

The Eiffel Tower was the tallest structure in the world. How long did it hold this record?

A. 10 months   B. 41 years

C. 106 years   D. 215 years

True or False

You can sneeze with your eyes open.

ISBN: 978-1-897457-77-1

Answer:

A. a giant storm

This giant storm has lasted for hundreds of years.

Answer:

B. 41 years

Answer:

false

It uses 95% of its energy to produce heat and only 5% to produce light.

Answer:

false

You can never sneeze with your eyes open.

ISBN: 978-1-897457-77-1

True or False

You have almost 100 000 kilometres of blood vessels in your body.

What makes an eggshell so strong?

A. its dome shape

B. its egg white

C. its material

Which soil contains the most organic matter?

A. light grey soil

B. yellow soil

C. dark brown soil

Where is the largest muscle in your body?

A. leg

B. chest

C. arm

D. bum

ISBN: 978-1-897457-77-1

Answer:

true

This may be hard to fathom, especially when the circumference of the Earth is a little over 40 000 kilometres.

Answer:

A. its dome shape

The dome shape distributes a force exerted at the top of the eggshell to all parts of the eggshell evenly.

Answer:

C. dark brown soil

The darker the soil is, the more organic matter it contains.

Answer:

D. bum

This largest muscle on your bum is called the gluteus maximus.

ISBN: 978-1-897457-77-1

What is the heaviest internal organ in your body?

A. heart

B. skin

C. brain

D. liver

True or False

In our solar system, Saturn is the only planet that has rings around it.

Our Earth has one moon. How many moons does Jupiter have?

A. 3

B. 63

C. 630

The chance of a house getting struck by lightning is less than 0.5%. About how many times does the CN Tower get struck each year?

A. 2   B. 75

C. 5000   D. 9000

ISBN: 978-1-897457-77-1

Answer:

D. liver

Skin is the heaviest organ of a human body, but it is not an internal organ.

Answer:

false

Jupiter, Uranus, and Neptune also have rings, but they are not as spectacular as those of Saturn.

Answer:

B. 63

Jupiter is the planet with the most moons in the solar system.

Answer:

B. 75

The CN Tower gets struck a lot more often than other structures due to its height and the lightning rod at the top.

ISBN: 978-1-897457-77-1

Which is the nearest star to the Earth?

A. the North Star

B. the sun

C. the moon

No cells can be viewed without a microscope.

There are trees that are taller than a 15-storey building.

What is the hottest temperature recorded in Canada?

A. 30°C

B. 45°C

C. 60°C

Answer:

B. the sun

The moon is near the Earth but it is not a star and the North Star is not in our solar system.

Answer:

true

Trees are the largest kind of plant.

Answer:

false

Though most cells are microscopic, some cells can be seen with the naked eye. An egg's yolk is a large single cell.

Answer:

B. 45°C

This temperature was recorded in Saskatchewan in 1937.

ISBN: 978-1-897457-77-1

Where do you find the smallest bone in your body?

A. toe
B. jaw
C. ear
D. finger

True or False

All the shining dots we see in the night sky are stars.

Which star is the hottest?

A. a yellow star
B. a blue star
C. a red star

True or False

Some planets emit light and some reflect light.

Answer:

C. ear

This bone in the human body is called the stirrup, and it is in your middle ear.

Answer:

false

Some of them are planets, like Venus and Jupiter, and others are satellites.

Answer:

B. a blue star

A star with a temperature of about 28 600°C appears to be blue, a star at 6000°C appears yellow, and one at 2500°C appears red.

Answer:

false

No planets emit light. They only reflect light. Only stars, like our sun, emit light.

ISBN 978-1-897457-77-1

True or False

Mars appears to be reddish because it is a very hot planet.

About how much of your body's energy does your brain consume?

A. 5%
B. 50%
C. 20%
D. 75%

True or False

Kids have more bones in their bodies than adults.

Which of the following is the longest bridge in Canada?

A. Confederation Bridge

B. Lions Gate Bridge

C. Broadway Bridge

ISBN: 978-1-897457-77-1

Answer:

false

Mars appears to be reddish because of the iron oxide in its soil.

Answer:

true

There are 206 bones in an adult human's body and 300 in a baby's body. As kids get older, some of their bones fuse together.

Answer:

C. 20%

Though your brain accounts for about 2% of your body weight, it uses 20% of your energy.

Answer:

A. Confederation Bridge

This bridge is 12.9 km long and connects Prince Edward Island with New Brunswick.

ISBN: 978-1-897457-77-1

True or False

The longest covered bridge is in Canada.

True or False

The Earth is older than the moon.

Where would you find a cricket's ears?

A. on its head

B. on its chest

C. on its front legs

D. crickets have no ears

Oxygen condenses into liquid if it is cold enough. What colour is its liquid form?

A. pale blue

B. white

C. light brown

Answer:

true

Hartland Bridge in Hartland, New Brunswick, is the world's longest covered bridge.

Answer:

true

The Earth is 200 million years older than the moon.

Answer:

C. on its front legs

Answer:

A. pale blue

Oxygen condenses into a pale blue liquid at -183°C.

ISBN: 978-1-897457-77-1

Where does sound travel the fastest?

A. in air
B. in space
C. in water

True or False

Most planets have no moons.

True or False

The substance that makes up an eggshell can also be found in a human tooth.

The Rogers Centre has a fully retractable roof. How long does it take to open this roof?

A. 2 seconds
B. 20 minutes
C. 2 hours

Answer:

C. in water

Sound travels faster in water than in air and it cannot travel in space because there is no air.

Answer:

true

This substance is calcium.

Answer:

false

All planets have moons except Mercury and Venus.

Answer:

B. 20 minutes

ISBN: 978-1-897457-77-1

True or False

The sun rises in the east and the moon rises in the west.

Do flying squirrels actually fly?

How many living organisms are there on the surface of your skin?

A. none

B. several thousands

C. several trillions

True or False

Diamond dissolves in a strong acid.

Answer:

false

Both the sun and the moon rise in the east and set in the west.

Answer:

No, they do not.

They can float like parachutes, but they cannot fly like birds.

Answer:

C. several trillions

There are over 1000 species of bacteria living all over your skin. Don't worry, though. Most are harmless, and some even help you by protecting you against bad bacteria.

Answer:

false

Only intense heat can destroy a diamond.

ISBN: 978-1-897457-77-1